Some
Shropshire
Gardens
revisited

LOGASTON PRESS
Little Logaston Woonton Almeley
Herefordshire HR3 6QH
logastonpress.co.uk

First published by Logaston Press 2005
Copyright © Barbara and Alan Palmer (text and photographs)

ISBN 1 904396 34 8

Set in Garamond by Logaston Press
Cover and book design by Eve Perloff
and printed in Great Britain by Cromwell Press Ltd,
Trowbridge, Wiltshire

Pictures:
Page 1: From Millichope Park and 63 Belle Vue Road
Page 3: Hodnet Hall
Page 4: (Top left to right) Little Heldre, Bitterley Court;
(Bottom left to right) Jinlye Cottage, The Wrekin Rose Garden
Page 5: (Top left to right) The Mount Cottage, Acton Round;
(Bottom left to right) Lower Hall, Preen Manor
Page 8: The laburnam tunnel at Swallow Hayes

Some
Shropshire Gardens
revisited

Barbara and Alan Palmer

Logaston Press

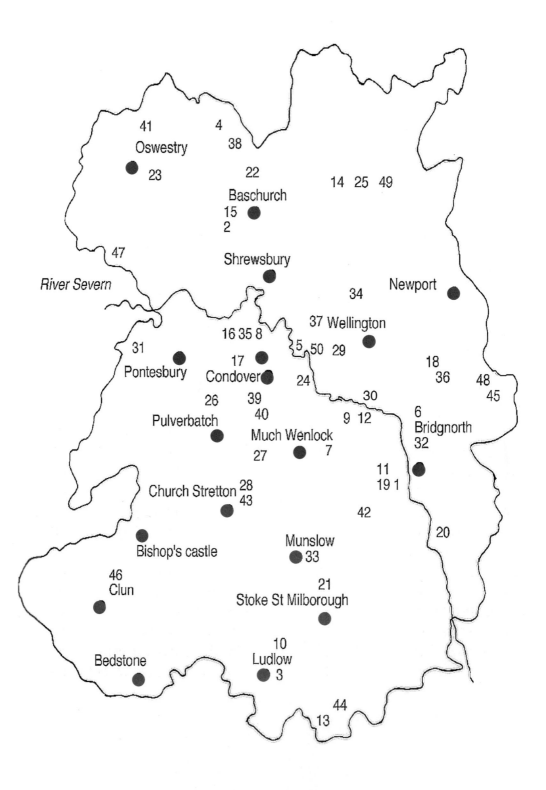

Outline map of the County of Shropshire showing locations
of the gardens described in this book

CONTENTS

The Laburnam Tunnel at Swallow Hayes

Introduction

Several years ago we wrote and photographed a book on Shropshire gardens, a very personal view of a diverse and eclectic selection. So why another book covering the same ground? Well, the first one was completed fourteen years ago and is now out of date. Many gardens we visited are no longer open or have changed out of all recognition. Conversely, some of the more important continue to delight, and we have tried to view them in a different season to point up other facets of their beauty.

A great many gardening books exhibit a tendency to be about important gardens around grand houses, appearing to have little to do with the average sized plot in suburbia. For this reason we deliberately sought out some of the smaller and more intimate, though all but two of the gardens are open, even if only for a few times a year. The grand has not been neglected however, with most of the major gardens covered.

Shropshire is a large and diverse county bordering on eight others — three Welsh — and is close to populous areas such as Birmingham and Wolverhampton. It continues to be a largely rural landscape however, especially where the boundary is between Herefordshire, Cheshire and Wales. This diversity is reflected in the gardens visited, and I can honestly say that no two are alike, from the suburbs of Telford, to rolling acres around country mansions of the highest architectural value. Sometimes in fact, the houses were almost as interesting as the gardens, and in all the best, most coherent schemes, played an important part in the overall picture. Shropshire is one of the 'black and white' counties, but also boasts excellent sandstone quarries at Grinshill, a stone used in some houses, as well as many classic, Georgian, red-brick buildings although brick use was rare until the industrial revolution.

There were many surprises in the two years it took to produce this book, not the least being the consistently high standard of design, maintenance and sheer beauty in the gardens visited, though Shropshire has always been credited with a reputation for horticultural excellence. This extends from the great gardens landscaped by famous names in the past, such as Repton and Capability Brown, through Shrewsbury's flower show at The Quarry (one of the first), Percy Thrower — an early television gardening star, to the present world renowned David Austin Roses.

A canard disproved seemed to be Shropshire's reputation as a 'cold county'. We were genuinely amazed at the number of tender plants now flourishing out of doors in both town and country plots. Thankfully, the current mania for decking and 'garden makeovers' has, as yet, had little influence on Shropshire's green acres. We were also intrigued by the fact that although Shropshire can legitimately be called 'wet', being a county rich in canals and rivers, including the Severn, Perry, Teme and Corve, to say nothing of its own miniature Lake District, and although many of the more important parks contain a large lake, only Hodnet and Lower Hall, Worfield, have really extensive water gardens.

Finally, may we thank the owners of the fifty gardens visited for their unfailing courtesy, hospitality and patience. Especially those who, because of adverse weather conditions, had to be bothered several times.

Barbara and Alan Palmer
March 2005

Acton Round • Morville

A large country garden surrounding an early Georgian house, with
well designed borders and fascinating follies. Open under the National Gardens Scheme,
see Yellow Book

Visitors approach Acton Round along a narrow, tortuous lane. Turning one of its lethal blind corners the house suddenly appears before you, architecturally distinguished, yet welcoming, its early Georgian symmetry made less austere by huge trees and clustering farm buildings in the same subtle orange brick as the house. The warm terracotta shade of the front is further enhanced by a line of *Euphorbia wulfenii* in acid green close up against the walls, and a formal garden consisting of a clipped, circular yew rondel, shaved lawn, and an ancient *Robinia pseudoacacia* dominating the front elevation. This tree must be hundreds of years old; although the genus is noted for fast growth.

Acton Round Hall has an interesting history. It was built in 1713 for Sir Whitmore Acton by the Smith brothers of Warwick, then, shortly afterwards, abandoned for almost two hundred years. It was inhabited again in 1918 and, as a result, the main building is very much as the Smith brothers envisaged, with very few alterations. The present owners began building and planting twenty years ago, finding only mature trees and some yew hedges dating from the 1930s. The layout is formal, as befits the restrained design of the house, but with gloriously profuse planting throughout and a wealth of follies, statues and arches in the 'Gothick' style, mostly originating from Wood House, Tettenhall, which was demolished some time ago. It is hard to imagine them now in a more suitable setting.

The many walls and pillared gates which together with the clipped yew hedges divide the garden, were built more recently, using brick salvaged from demolished farm buildings and, as a result, appear contemporary with the house. At the rear (the garden front) the ground slopes gently up from the house and is divided into a small terraced area with steps up to the main lawn. Across the grass and up further steps, a wide green path leads under a tall pillared entrance to the vegetable garden, a weathered statue of a hunter providing a focal point. To each side of the path are areas of rough grass filled with early bulbs, while intriguing views of gate arches topped by stone dogs, a pagoda and an obelisk, can be glimpsed behind trees and through gaps in the hedges.

A walk around the garden begins under the large eucalyptus which shades the entrance, here one's eye is immediately caught by the perfect little 'Gothick' summerhouse in brick, with church windows of sandstone. It is close up against the wall and covered in climbers, including a bright pink rose which somehow manages not to clash with the brickwork. Corners of the mixed herbaceous and shrub borders are marked by silver leaf pears and the dark red *Prunus cerasifera* 'Pissardii'. The planting around the aforementioned 'Dog Gate' is a *tour de force* — more euphorbias, *Senecio greyii* (a huge bush) and *Anthemis cupaniana*. Green, grey and white blending perfectly against the warm brickwork.

The overall impression may be one of formality, but everywhere this is offset by self-sown aquilegia, honesty, Welsh poppies and ladies mantle. (The owner admits that hoes are banned at Acton Round.) The vegetable garden is an object lesson in 'how to do it' and is the only place where help is

employed. It is completely hidden from the ornamental garden by a high wall, and must be one of the very best that we have encountered. The rows of beans, peas and other vegetables are laid out in military precision, without a weed to be seen.

A path overhung with *Viburnum opulus*, the snowball tree, leads off to a wilder, woodland area laid out in 1986, but most visitors now head for the Japanese pagoda, just in sight over the trees. This is a modern addition, but perfectly in keeping with the rest of the garden as it inhabits a site to the side of the garden proper overlooking the tennis court. It is of some height, and consists of three tiers with steps up to a viewing platform. I loved it, and can't think of a pleasanter place to drink tea on a sunny afternoon.

There is a small enclosed formal garden in this area, which also reflects the Japanese theme, being centred on a bronze incense burner atop a stone pillar. It must be either a shi-shi or a toad, but in any event is an unqualified success, surrounded by neatly clipped box, herbaceous borders and dwarf conifers. Once again, the formality is offset by foxgloves, Welsh poppies and forget-me-nots which have obviously chosen their own positions, while convallaria force a way through every crack in the paving.

Although many of the plantings are tried and true cottage favourites, such as hardy geraniums, euphorbias, oriental poppies and delphiniums, there are also many unusual plants on show, including a superb mature Judas tree, always a talking point, with the small purple blooms growing directly out of the stem. Also the rare, yellow-bronze form of polemonium, as well as the ornamental thistle *Morrina longifolia*. The latter has long, toothed leaves, with beautiful pink and white flowers growing in whorls up the stem and prefers a moist, but well-drained border in full sun.

How can one go wrong with a garden like Acton Round? The setting would be hard to better, surrounded by glorious countryside. The house is an architectural gem, the gardens a well designed mixture of formal and informal, setting it off to perfection.

Adcote School · Little Ness

A Norman Shaw house with extensive parkland and gardens.
Open under the National Gardens Scheme, see Yellow Book

Adcote is a garden of elegant simplicity designed around a Norman Shaw house; the typical, faux Tudor, Arts and Crafts design in pinkish-grey local sandstone contrasting beautifully with the lush green of the surrounding park. It became a school for girls in 1927 and in 1960 was awarded Grade 1 listed building status. The original owners were the Darbys of Ironbridge fame and the gardens appear to be contemporary with the house. Their chief glory are the mature trees, especially the cedars and giant beech underplanted with rhododendrons in all shades of mauve and pink. The Darbys followed the Victorian tradition of being great hoarders, and built up large botanical collections, including a herbarium which has recently been given to the University of Cambridge.

The classic view is at the rear of the house, where one looks back along a ruler straight path bordered by clipped hedges and standard, shaved, Portuguese laurel, the only touch of colour when we visited coming from massed rhododendrons to the right of the path. In case this is too severe, one turns and is faced by a yew 'cottage', complete with chimney. Whimsy is hard to blend into a formal setting, but somehow this folly fits perfectly. A great square of grass to the right of the path, entered through an arch in the hedge and partially surrounded by high walls, was, I am sure, once the vegetable garden, or perhaps a box parterre, which would of course echo the Tudor theme.

The front of the house has a gravelled courtyard, giving a far more intimate feel, though the entrance door is imposing, and there is a remarkable window of enormous size to the right. Here viburnum bushes, the flat, pure white 'Mariesii', and the round, aptly named 'Snowball', peep over the hardstone walls softening the effect, while abies show open fingers of pale new growth. In fact, all of the many conifers in the park are well placed, the flatness of yellow junipers set against strong verticals in darker green. Other fine trees include red flowered horse chestnuts, *Aesculus x carnea* and blue cedars

Cedrus atlantica glauca, showing that even without extensive flower beds there need be no lack of colour.

A lawn slopes downwards away from the side of the house, approached by mysterious paths redolent with the scent of the common yellow azalea still unbeatable for perfume. Here there are huge variegated hollies and more ancient cedars undermined by rabbits and badgers. Massed rhododendrons, this time the old fashioned mauve, contrast with the dark purple of the copper beech. This rhododendron has naturalised itself in many parts of the British Isles and become almost a weed in north Wales. Its bright flowers are very beautiful *en masse*, however, and are a feature on the hillsides in May and June. If you want a better form, try the double *R. ponticum* 'Flore Pleno'. The yew hedge in this part of the garden is topped by cheeky, carved squirrels, eternally facing one another and again, I am sure, part of the original garden plan.

There is a formal border close to the house (one of the few in the garden) against a terrace wall planted with shrubs. The grey sandstone is a perfect backing for roses: 'Roseraie de l' Hay' in pink; the yellow leaf orange blossom, *Philadelphus coronarius*

'Aureus'; red berberis, and the dark purple leaf *Weigela florida* 'Foliis Purpureis'. Wildlife obviously does well at Adcote, the eaves of the great house proving a paradise for swallows and house martins.

The inside of the house echoes the grandeur of the exterior elevations, with an imposing Great Hall used as a main living room when the Darbys were in residence, and is full of typical Tudor features. There is a crown-pin roof with huge stone arches and a Minstrel's Gallery, but the eye is drawn to a hooded stone fireplace similar to the ones seen in ruined, mediaeval, Welsh castles. Most of the original furniture, which also followed the Arts and Crafts style, has long since disappeared, (some can be viewed at Dudmaston, Quatt, see page 50). There are still interesting reminders of the past however, such as the wonderful de Morgan tiles on the fireplace in the Library, (once the withdrawing room), and also produced at Ironbridge.

Adcote is surrounded by beautiful countryside, which almost becomes part of the garden with views over rolling fields to far away 'blue remembered hills'. Setting, garden and house combine to make an unforgetable picture.

Angel Gardens • Clee Hill

A new garden on an old site with many interesting water features.

Open under the National Gardens Scheme, see Yellow Book

Although the house at Angel Gardens is three hundred years old the garden is very new. Four years ago the owners were faced with a sloping, undulating field, and literally sculpted it into the shapes they required with a bulldozer. They state that barely an inch of the ground remains with the same topography they found, digging out a boggy area at the bottom to create a magnificent large pond — the surplus soil used as an earth dam — and landscaping flat areas for sitting, vegetables and a tennis court. They used immense care and much thought to preserve the breathtaking views over four counties as far as the Long Mynd, also replacing top soil so that the many interesting trees and shrubs would have the best possible start.

A ruined cottage near the bottom of the garden's one and a half acres was raided for the blocks of stone utilised to terrace the slope behind the house and to construct the ha-ha in front, so that nothing interrupts the view. Using old stone found on site not only cuts down the expense of extensive terracing, but ensures that the walls are perfectly in keeping with existing old buildings, and makes for an harmonious whole.

Planting is of course still immature, but the garden does have some old native trees, including a row of field maples, once part of a hedge, with picturesque twisted trunks. *Acer campestre*, also known as the hedge maple, is a fine tree for any garden, taking a long time to reach an unmanageable height and spread, and turning a glowing, butter-yellow in the autumn. It is far less temperamental than *Acer palmatum*, the Japanese maple, for an exposed position, as well as being bone hardy in late frosts.

The large pond (or small lake) dominates the garden, and the owners have built a Japanese style summer house overlooking it, with decking actually overhanging the water. Where the lake narrows, a rustic bridge provides a short cut back to the house. The lake has no liner, as the soil is heavy clay, but there is an ingenious system whereby the overflow is led by pipe to a further smaller pond lower down the slope, stored, and then pumped up to fill the top lake in the event of a drought. Being on the

side of Clee Hill however, and with the house once called Springfield, I should think this is an unlikely occurrence. I asked how long the pond, twelve metres deep in some places, took to fill. The answer was very slowly at first, then, after a dramatic downpour, very quickly!

The owners of Angel Gardens prefer an uncluttered surface of reflections, and have eschewed water lilies and other deep water plants, though the edges play host to many damp loving herbaceous perennials such as mimulus, flag iris, hosta, astilbe, day lilies and *Alchemilla mollis* or ladies mantle. The latter's fluffy green flowers and beautiful leaves are much beloved by flower arrangers, and a real cottage garden favourite.

An open, unclaustrophobic feel is also preferred in the main garden, with sweeping vistas and no attempt to confine the area into 'rooms' with hedges. I think the owners have chosen their style well. All gardens should make the best use of favourable conditions, taking advantage of what is already there and their cue from the surrounding countryside — in the case of Angel Gardens, the boggy site and the magnificent views.

Much planting and digging is still going on, and the owners showed me a box of china dug up on site, some pieces being mediaeval slip ware. There has obviously been a house in the same place for many hundreds of years, the present typical Shropshire stone cottage dating back to the seventeenth century. It looks as if it has grown from the bank, cosily situated with its back to the hill.

I loved the pretty terrace at the rear of the house, well planted with ground covering alpines. Nothing rare or difficult, but all carefully chosen to blend in shape and colour. Lysimachia, pink and white saxifraga, helichrysum — the sun roses — and prostrate hebes, with an occasional dwarf, upright conifer to add another dimension. This bed is echoed by one of heathers and conifers further down the slope and another of taller perennials such as lupins, phlox and veronicas.

Walking around the garden on a beautiful day accompanied by the gentle music from wind chimes, I visualised it in five or ten years time when fully mature. I think that it will bring much joy to the owners and their visitors.

April Cottage · Ellesmere

A timber-framed cottage reputed to be the oldest house in Ellesmere,

with a wildlife garden overlooking the Mere. Open occasionally for the benefit of the local church

Situated half way up a steep hill between a mound on which a motte-and-bailey timber castle built in 1120 once stood and the mediaeval church (heavily restored in the nineteenth century), April Cottage is believed to be the oldest house in Ellesmere. Its owners bravely took on a complete wreck, as the cottage had been uninhabited for seven years. Their reward was a unique setting with glorious views of the Mere and the surrounding countryside. It came, however, with a challenging sloping site bereft of anything useful except some neglected fruit trees, and full of much to strike terror into a gardener's heart, including nettles, ground elder, brambles and the dreaded Japanese knotweed. Gardeners plagued with the latter may be interested to know that it was only defeated by injecting weed killer directly into the stem, then instantly pulling up any new shoots that appeared.

I vividly remember one of the owners of April Cottage telling me that she 'had one more garden left in her' when they moved in fourteen years ago, and that this time it was going to be a wildlife garden. A wildlife garden it may be, but there are many other facets to this interesting site.

The black and white building fronts directly onto a narrow sunken lane, with the church towering above and visible from almost all parts of the garden. Fortunately the lane is little used by motor vehicles, and in true cottage style the verge in front has been cultivated. When we visited the wisteria was fading, but roses, hardy geranium and colourful ground cover plants were taking its place.

Most of the flowers and shrubs in the garden are chosen for ease of cultivation and usefulness to birds, bees and other insects, but an extraordinary buddleia close up against

a sheltering wall proved to be the rare *Buddleia colvilei,* a native of the Sikkim Himalaya. It is very vigorous, with leaves like an ordinary *B. davidii,* but the flowers, in rich pink with a paler throat, are individually huge and borne in long panicles, making it one of the most distinctive and beautiful of all the buddleia family. It appears to be much hardier than first thought, but for safety is best planted against a high wall in a sheltered position. The owners of April Cottage have often tried to propagate it, but cuttings are reluctant to take and it does not ripen seed.

Inside the garden proper the whole area has been planned around the view. A J.C.B. was brought in early to level the area close to the house, and this now consists mostly of island beds with gravel walks between. They are all circular, following the pattern of the old castle which was ringed with a variety of defences. Plants again are in cottage style: *Nepeta x faassenii,* a blue aromatic haze tumbling over the edges onto paths, hardy geranium and primroses, although one bed is of heathers for winter colour.

I loved the way the owners had made use of all the old bricks and paving stones dug up in the garden, incorporating them into steps and paths. Some superb tiles with patterns resembling mediaeval ones which can be seen in old abbeys and castles have been used in an outdoor room, others are reputed to have come from the church when it was restored by Sir George Gilbert Scott in 1847.

There is still very little flat ground at April Cottage, so the owners have built what they describe as 'Charlie Dimmock' decking at the very top of the garden with steps up, complete with garden room and electric kettle. From this height the view over the Mere is even better, and appropriately for a vista over water, is known as the 'Upper Deck'.

The old orchard is a paradise for wildlife, and here the owners merely mow around the wild flowers leaving seed heads alone and planting shrubs with winter berries such as the guelder rose. It is hard to define where the garden ends and the surrounding woodland begins. This is a deliberate ploy, as much of the woodland close to the Mere has been designated a nature reserve, and the amorphous boundaries encourage squirrels, badgers and other mammals to come into the garden.

To garden in such a fascinating place, with history in the shape of the castle and church, the Mere and wildlife so close, seems my idea of perfection.

Attingham Park • Atcham

One of the grandest country houses in Shropshire, surrounded by superb parkland laid out
by Humphry Repton. Owned by the National Trust and open frequently.

Attingham Park is the archetypal grand country house, with Ionic columns, lavish interiors, groves of magnificent trees, a picturesque river and an unrivalled situation in lush countryside. The house was built for Noel Hill, the first Lord Berwick in 1782–85 and designed by George Steuart, a contemporary of Robert Adam. It is interesting to note that an earlier house on the site called Tern Hall was not demolished, but incorporated into the new building. The entire estate covers around 3,700 acres and the first person to attempt a transformation from what was described in 1784 as 'ugly grounds', was Thomas Leggett. He planted over 20,000 trees and altered the formal setting of Tern Hall to a more fashionable, open parkland, containing groups of trees strategically placed, with others used as screens at newly extended boundaries.

Humphry Repton, who was commissioned by the second Lord Berwick, had an excellent legacy to build on and made the most of it, producing a gentle, very natural landscape, and bringing the River Tern with its bridges into the picture. Leggett's thick tree plantings, now mature, were judiciously pruned, creating vistas from the house to the Wrekin, and giving the impression that Lord Berwick's land was without boundaries.

A book on Shropshire gardens is hardly the place to write about interiors, but mention must be made of Attingham's elegant rooms. These contain an interesting collection of furniture, mostly in the French style favoured by the Prince Regent, and are as dramatic and grandiose as the great portico outside. The picture gallery was designed by John Nash, and still contains some significant works, although much has been dispersed in forced sales throughout the years. (Thomas, the second Lord Berwick, was declared bankrupt in 1827.)

One approaches Attingham today from the village of Atcham and the old A5 — the latter incidentally rerouted by Noel Hill — through an imposing, arched entrance also designed by John Nash. Repton was fond of hiding a large house behind a clump of trees so that it appeared suddenly on rounding a corner. At Attingham, a group of oaks screen the house, so that the impression one gets when eventually the huge building with its tall portico and flanking wings comes into view is all the more dramatic. It dominates the scene, the strong uprights of the grey Ionic columns set off by a group of dark green cedar close to the east wing. Just one of these big trees is usually enough to fill a large garden, but at Attingham a magnificent grove of mature trees between the river and the house are perfectly placed and just the right scale. Anything less would be overwhelmed by the architecture, but the cedars hold their own.

The River Tern was straightened by Repton and a weir built by Nash, but this was swept away in floods and the river has reverted to its original meandering course. I cannot believe it once looked any better than it does today, the bridges, now weathered so that they seem part of the landscape, forming focal points.

The garden proper, enclosed within the ha-ha to the front of the house, has seen many changes over the years, once encompassing a bowling green as well as formal terraces, even, in latter years, an Italian garden. The National Trust have wisely reinstated Repton's open parkland landscape, which so suits the drama of the great house, concentrating on the wonderful trees and sweeping vistas.

The woodland at the rear of the house contains many native trees, a delight in the autumn and carpeted with snowdrops and bluebells in early spring. Exotics are not neglected however, with a circle of *Gleditsia triacanthos*, or honey locust, a tall, elegant tree with frond-like leaves and long brown seed pods in a good season; as well as many azaleas, rhododendrons and camellias.

The walled garden is some way from the main building, as was the fashion in Repton's time. It was originally planted with vegetables for the house, as well as a quantity of fruit trees and flowers for cutting. An interesting point is that the late Percy Thrower, one of the first TV gardeners, used the walled garden to demonstrate the art of vegetable culture in some of his early programmes. I thought the old timber bee house, also in this part of the garden, quite fascinating. It once contained sixteen straw skeps or bee hives, and, as it used to stand in the orchard, must have contributed much to the pollination of the fruit.

Attingham Park is gardening on a grand scale, and there is little in the form of flower beds. The back of the house, where old Tern Hall once stood, is now an enclosed garden however, and the autumn beds, hugging vast walls hung with Virginia creeper, are full of Michaelmas daisies, golden rod and the hot colours of heleniums. Earlier in the season, yellow old English roses, cardoons and hemerocallis, or the day lilies, take their place.

There is an impressive stable block built around a courtyard also designed by George Steuart, as well as a Deer Park. The deer are part of the landscape, and were beloved by the last Lord Berwick who visited them daily when in residence. They are believed to be descended from wild deer which lived in the area when the park was first enclosed.

Attingham cannot be appreciated in one visit but must be viewed in all seasons of the year, preferably when wearing stout shoes to fully enjoy the extensive walks through beautiful woodlands, perhaps at their best on sunny autumn days. Or even in early spring when the trees are still bare, snowdrops cover the ground and the great house can be seen in all its glory from many different points in the park.

Badger Farmhouse · Badger

*A large farmhouse garden with over three hundred varieties of daffodils and narcissi
in an orchard setting. Open under the National Gardens Scheme, see Yellow Book*

If you visit Badger Farmhouse in the springtime it is difficult to dismiss Wordsworth's famous poem to the daffodil from one's mind; because in this garden they really do come in 'A crowd, a host of golden daffodils'. And not just golden; there are over three hundred varieties in the three-acre garden, mostly planted in grass among fruit trees. I had never realised before just what an enormous variation there is in the daffodil and narcissi family, from the small, pale daffodils immortalised by Wordsworth and still growing wild in the Lake District, to the elaborate, highly coloured modern hybrids seen in garden centres today.

Most of the daffodils at Badger Farmhouse are planted in large groups of one variety under trees in light shade, in my opinion the perfect way to set off this quintessential British flower. There are groups in every shade of cream, some with darker trumpets, some with pale, as well as rich chrome yellows, even one clump with a distinctly pinkish tinge; though I must admit a preference for the pure white, older forms, such as 'Mount Hood'. The trees are mainly what remains of an ancient orchard — apple, cherry, pear and plum, with characteristic gnarled and twisted trunks, some overgrown with green lichen. Few of the daffodil varieties are known, there could even be very old cultivars contemporary with the house, a Georgian brick building dating from 1779. All look exquisite, however, with their green grass background, especially a gorgeous lemon with just a shade darker trumpet nestling under a large *Magnolia x soulangiana* in rich pink.

Paths in the garden tend to the wild and grassy, though some are defined by old,

well-clipped box hedges, and a wide path leading from the front of the house ends in an urn used as a focal point.

The owners of Badger Farmhouse are comparatively new to gardening and are learning 'on the job', so to speak. Their aim is a child-friendly garden with not too much maintenance (though they do have some help) while keeping an open, uncomplicated aspect. Soil is a very light sand, which obviously suits the bulbs well. I suspect that not much dividing and thinning takes place, there are just too many, but all are flowering magnificently. It is of course essential to use a little fertiliser on most bulbs growing in grass, and to allow the leaves to die down naturally if you want to keep up the flowering performance over many seasons.

Serious farming was abandoned at Badger Farmhouse ten years ago, but fortunately the buildings, including a superb range of old barns, were sympathetically converted into houses, all separated by tall brick walls of reclaimed brick. These provide excellent places to grow climbers, including many roses. Large island beds in the main garden contain groups of camellias and rhododendrons under-planted with yet more daffodils, as well as blue notes coming from clumps of muscari and hyacinth, while the wide, undulating lawns are dotted with shrubs and tall mature trees. Of special note are the cedar and many interesting picea, as well as deciduous sycamores and other, rarer specimens.

I mentioned that the aim is a child-friendly garden, and a small paddock has been set aside as a children's playground, with trampoline, climbing frame and tyre swings. There is also space to kick a ball

being thinned out and hedges — one the owner states is over twenty feet high — are receiving a cut back, while a wooden gazebo is being rebuilt. A row of tall Scots pine has been retained, however, to provide shelter against prevailing winds.

There are herbaceous beds close to the house for later colour, but the fruit blossom and the daffodils give this garden its unique early spring *raison d'être*. Though I couldn't help wondering, come the autumn, what on earth the owners do with all the fruit.

without damaging the flowers. I liked the way this area was part of the garden and yet screened from it by shrubs and a hedge.

The many mature trees and bushes make the garden a paradise for birds — an old fruit tree is second only to an oak in its usefulness to wildlife. Birds of course can become a problem when it comes to vegetable cultivation and the plot set aside at Badger Farmhouse is well protected by nets, the only way to get a worthwhile crop.

The garden is undergoing some change and renovation at the moment. Trees are

The Bayliff's House · Broseley

A Tudor house with a large plantsman's garden set in three acres of woodland.

Open under the National Gardens Scheme, see Yellow Book

The Bayliff's House sits in the centre of a clearing among the thick woods that clothe the steep hill leading down to the River Severn and Ironbridge. When we visited the garden during one of the most spectacularly colourful autumns for many years (2003) it was a green oasis in a sea of brown and gold. Not that the one-and-a-half acre garden was without its own fireworks in the shape of dogwoods, Rhus typhina, flowering cherries and Michaelmas daisies. I must admit that I had not realised before how very colourful the cherries can be in their autumn dress.

But — to begin at the beginning. The house is a Tudor gem dating from 1672, and with a date stone to prove it. It is contemporary with nearby Benthall Hall (see page 26) and was, as its name suggests, the bailiff of the Benthall estates abode. During the past three hundred and fifty years however, it has also served as both a workhouse and a private dwelling. As one would expect in a house of this age, it appears to grow out of the landscape, and is built of the same mellow grey sandstone as its up-market neighbour Benthall Hall.

The present owners have owned and loved the house and its garden for twenty-seven years, finding only lawns, trees and ninety-two hybrid tea roses when they moved in. In its favour the situation, hidden amongst the trees, is glorious, while the soil is a fast draining neutral loam that will grow almost anything. The owners had made two previous gardens in Yorkshire, catching the bug from a gardening friend and at first using the garden largely as relaxing therapy. Interest grew, however, and with the acquisition of The Bayliff's House, serious plans were made which over the years have gradually come to fruition.

The front of the house faces woodland and paddock with the garden proper to the sides and rear of the building, although it is hard to define where the garden ends and the woods and wild garden begin. Paths from the back lead into the trees at several points, the edges blurred by drifts of bulbs in spring and early summer.

On the south side of the house formality reigns, with tailored yew hedges confining the garden, together with paths, lawns and flower beds. The original concept was to grow only plants found in this country in the seventeenth century, but the owner is a plantswoman and simply couldn't resist the temptation to widen her palette. The whole area works well, keeping the essential formality which so suits the house, while using the more modern idea of profuse planting with much variety of texture and a mixture of shrubs and perennials. The overall colour scheme throughout the year is a soft yellow. Although all the hybrid tea roses were removed, shrub roses are a favourite of the owners, and *Rosa cantabrigiensis*, which has single yellow flowers as well as leaves which turn a delightful glowing gold in the autumn, fits this part of the garden to perfection.

There are many good clematis in the garden, usually grown through vigorous early flowering shrubs to extend their season of interest. One in particular is rarely seen and very tricky to grow, namely, *Clematis* 'Gravetye Beauty'. I can only describe it as a cherry-red four pointed star, which looks in bud like a refined tulip. It flowers very late, sometimes not getting going until September, and is the despair of many gardeners. I have yet to find the ideal situation in any garden I have ever made. At The Bayliff's House it drapes itself across a gold lonicera bush, and was covered in flowers as well as many promising buds.

Most of the garden follows the natural lie of the land, and one climbs steps to the Silver and Gold Garden through a beautiful, especially commissioned, wrought-iron arch covered in a golden hop. If you only have room for one climber make it the golden hop, as it is superb in leaf and fruit, as well as drying particularly well. In contrast to 'Gravetye Beauty' it is also extremely easy to grow and propagate — you just dig up shoots with roots. The Gold and Silver Garden is at its best earlier in the year, but ballota; choisya — Mexican orange blossom — in its gold leaf form; yellow potentilla; marigolds and the small tree, *Malus* 'Golden Hornet', were still putting on a wonderful show, the silver plants in particular enjoying the dry weather and perfect drainage.

The garden has many superb pieces of sculpture, from a bronze abstract in the

south garden designed by Giuseppi Lund (he had a hand in the Queen Mother's gate at Hyde Park) to some wonderful 'found' pieces of water-worn wood reminiscent of Barbara Hepworth's famous rounded and holed sculptures.

The garden is still evolving, with a new summerhouse overlooking the revamped wild garden in the process of being built. This should also make a good hide to observe the wildlife with which the garden abounds — badgers, butterflies, deer, foxes, as well as uncountable birds, including such rarities as the green woodpecker.

No garden is perfect, and The Bayliffe's House is in a frost pocket, the owners stating they have decided to give up trying to grow hydrangeas. But one only has to note the ancient apple with its huge bunches of mistletoe, or the dogwood trees in autumn shades of pink, mauve, cream, pale orange and green, to know that it has many other charms to delight the true garden lover.

63 Belle Vue Road • Shrewsbury

A small, urban garden, packed with fascinating plants and holder of the National Collection

of convallaria or lily of the valley. Open occasionally for charity and by appointment.

Please telephone: 01743 272475 for details

Number 63 Belle Vue Road is a typical long, narrow, town garden, behind an early nineteenth-century terraced house. The plants, however, couldn't be more untypical. Perhaps the most extraordinary horticultural sight to be seen in Shropshire is the thirty-foot, roof-top skimming mimosa, *Acacia dealbata* which dominates the garden close to the house. This tree, a native of semi-tropical regions of Australia, is generally recommended for very temperate gardens in Cornwall, and then only against a south wall and close to the benign influence of the sea. To see one of this height, in perfect condition, a mass of pale yellow, scented flowers in March, seems little short of extraordinary in our cold inland county. It obviously had a good start in a sheltered sunny position, and probably some luck early on with mild winters; but even the owner is surprised at its ultimate height and continuing vigour.

The rest of the garden is simplicity itself, consisting of a straight, then curving path from one end of the garden to the other, ending in the utility area with compost, plant store and mini-greenhouse. There was once a lawn, but it was gradually eaten away over the fourteen years the owner has gardened on the site to allow more and more room for plants.

When we visited, the *Helleborus orientalis* were stealing the show, but many other treasures are to be found in all seasons of the year as you make your way down the narrow gravel and brick path. A favourite of mine, and easily overlooked, is the tiny green, *Hacquetia epipacti*, also the double primroses, difficult to keep in bare soil, but worth all the trouble of constant mulching and dividing. The convallaria were just breaking the surface of the ground, their green spears not yet in flower. There are not a great many forms, the best known — apart from the common, heavily scented white — being the double variety *C. majalis* 'Flore Pleno'; the pink, *C. m. var. rosea*; and perhaps the variegated leaf, *C. m. 'Albistriata'*. All these are fairly easy to get hold of from a good nursery, and will flourish in any shady, not too dry spot. Convallaria do have a mind of their own however, rather like snowdrops and Madonna lilies, and sometimes do not thrive in a particular position for no apparent reason. The best advice is to plant three plants in three different places; one at least should make it.

The owner of 63 Belle Vue Road has had no official horticultural training, but did work for many years at a large garden centre, as well as a florist, and this is reflected in the layout and choice of plants.

Although there are some trees in the garden, height in the middle portion comes from clumps of bamboo. The owner states that she loves everything about them, including the wind blowing through the leaves, and also approves the way one has total control over height and spread in a confined space. There is a *Paulownia tomentosa* at the end of the garden which flowers well providing there are no April frosts, but my eye was drawn to an enormous *Ceanothus coeruleus* 'Concha', not a variety that I am familiar with, but recommended as the very best blue by the owner. The size of the plant is astonishing. It is a true tree, with a well defined trunk, and cannot be described as a bush. Close by is an apricot, which not only

provides blossom, but fruit in such quantities that the owner gives them away to neighbours. There truly must be something in the soil at 63 Belle Vue, that 'something', was later revealed to be mushroom compost which is used as a mulch in the winter, all the home-made compost (contained in two alternate bins) being utilised for potting up.

Although the garden is too small for conifers, there are many evergreens for winter interest and to provide a background for the herbaceous perennials. I noted the fairly common *Sarcococca ruscifolia*, or Christmas box and the distinctly uncommon *Corgara* 'Golden King', a member of the pea family, with a hanging, bright yellow flower in early spring; as well as the evergreen currant, *Ribes speciosum*, which has tiny, crimson-red, dangling blooms.

Brick walls and tall wooden fences give privacy throughout the garden, but are completely hidden by climbers for most of the year — chiefly unusual roses such as the tiny 'Pompom de Paris', or *Rosa banksiae* 'Lutea', as well as many clematis. Later in the year peonies and aconitum take their place. The owner adores delphiniums, but they do not thrive and she finds monkshood a good substitute. A reliable and effective system of staking is essential if these plants are not to be beaten down, and I noted a group of bent canes awaiting use, which method the owner has found to be the most satisfactory in the confined space.

Care has to be taken that self-seeding plants do not get out of hand, but the somewhat rampant celandine family are tolerated in the rare double and pale cream forms, as are many unusual astrantias.

Somehow, room has been found for a small sitting out area in a sunny position close to the house, and there is a tiny front garden, also crowded with treasures. But it is the scent from the huge mimosa which lingers in the memory, as well as the unforgettable sight of its pale yellow flowers against the blue of the spring sky.

Benthall Hall • Broseley

An atmospheric, sixteenth-century stone house, with newly restored kitchen garden. Owned by the National Trust and open frequently in season. Please telephone: 01952 882159 for opening times

Benthall Hall is very much a sixteenth-century house, but some mystery hangs over its exact date of construction, tradition giving it as 1535. It is believed to have been extended later in the century when it became expedient to build hiding places, or priest holes, within the fabric of the house, and is now a beautiful, grey, sandstone building, with mullioned and transomed windows, fitting comfortably into the heavily wooded countryside above the Severn Gorge. Near the house, and clearly visible from many parts of the garden, is a church which could once have been a private chapel for the hall. There is a Saxon font inside, giving credence to the site's ancient origins, though both church and house were severely damaged during the civil wars, when the owner's son fought on the king's side.

The garden also has an interesting history, as George Maw — known in Victorian times as an important plant collector, especially the crocus genus — was for a time a tenant. Among the bulbs planted by Maw and now flowering annually at Benthall are *Crocus speciosus, C. pulchellus* and *C. nudiflorus*. In the woods around are many more, as well as native species. English bluebells for example, are followed by *Lilium martagon* growing abundantly beneath the trees in shades from pure white to dark crimson.

The terraces and rockeries which exist in the garden today are mostly the work of another tenant, Robert Bateman, whose father created the garden at Biddulph Grange. They have a definite Victorian air (in keeping with Biddulph Grange, surely the ultimate Victorian garden) but have now lost their formality completely, as they are almost invisible beneath lavender, hardy geraniums, dwarf campanulas and huge cistus bushes. Some structure does still exist in the shape of neatly clipped hedges and hollies, but these too overflow their allotted positions, billowing over paths and walls. Colour combinations in this part of the garden are superb, yellow roses under-planted with *Geranium* 'Johnson's Blue', or pink roses set against the grey sandstone walls.

An oblong pond is almost hidden by water lilies, while more hardy geraniums, this time *G.* 'Wargrave Pink' and *G. striatum*, as well as a scented, small, double orange-blossom, are sheltered by the wall of the house. There is an extraordinary sundial set in a circular raised bed covered in low spreading plants, while cobbled paths lead to another sundial and a seat, nicely placed for contemplating the roses or listening to the cooing of the doves from the nearby dovecote. There are many cottage favourites to be seen, such as edgings of *Alchemilla mollis and bergenia*, while apricot roses peep over a hedge of yellow potentilla and the rare *Paeonia suffruticosa* nestles against one of the many walls. All around great trees are visible: copper beech, sweet chestnut, oak, beech and lime, providing a muted green backdrop to the colour in the garden.

The formal south-east front of the house faces an oval patch of grass set in gravel, while the lawn, flanked by shrub and herbaceous beds, descends in a series of terraces to a ha-ha and a view. This is one of the few exposed areas in the whole plot, as cold winds blow from the north-east, and shelter belts of conifers and deciduous trees were planted in the 1960s. Notable trees at the top of the terraces include *Magnolia x soulangiana* 'Alba Superba' and *Dipteronia sinensis*, which has wonderful pinnate leaves, tiny flowers, and strange, winged, red-brown seeds in a good year.

The old vegetable garden is reached by a narrow path skirting the side of the house, and had not been developed when we last visited Benthall Hall nearly fourteen years ago. It is now a very important facet of the garden, and an absolute triumph of planting and design. The whole plot is enclosed by tall brick walls, with a central grassed area made up of neatly cut lawn containing fruit trees and patches of rough grass through which run mown paths. A glorious combination of fruit, vegetables, herbs and flowers are grown in close harmony, while a flagged path follows the walls around the plot. There are clematis-covered arches and a rose-hung bower with a seat, while a tiny pond almost disappears beneath a carpet of water lilies. A yellow theme was in evidence in the main body of this garden when we visited in late June, with golden hop, cream roses, *Philadelphus coronarius* 'Aureus', great stands of the common *Lysimachia punctata*, foxtail lilies, and a magnificent patch of *Iris wilsonii* in yellow and gold, all set off by clipped rounds of *Lonicera nitida* 'Baggessen's Gold'. There are hollyhocks and delphiniums close to rows of parsley, origanum and chives, all contained by old fashioned brick edging, while Victorian style glass cloches glint in the sun. Rudbeckias with black cone centres grow near to the green form of *Ruta graveolens*, now a rare sight as it has been almost completely superseded by *R.* 'Jackman's Blue'. Perhaps the most delightful touch of all is a seat beneath a canopy of roses within picking distance of a loganberry loaded with red fruit.

I always admired Benthall Hall gardens for their combination of historical ambience, trees and tradition, but the development of the vegetable garden has enabled them to claim a position as one of the most charming and distinctive in Shropshire.

Bitterley Court • Ludlow

A dignified, part Jacobean house, with a six-acre garden featuring rare trees and an ornamental kitchen garden. Open under the National Gardens Scheme, see Yellow Book

Villages in and around Clun in Shropshire are described in an old poem as 'the quietest places under the sun,' but I think that the countryside bordering Bitterley Court near Ludlow must come second or third in the list. The lanes are narrow, the bends tortuous, while the sight of an eleventh-century Norman church announces that you have arrived at your destination.

The garden is large, with the main theme uncluttered and simple, relying on magnificent trees and sweeping lawns for its visual impact. Bitterley Court itself is an important element in the design — a grand Jacobean house with a pedimented Georgian front. The main lawn faces this front and is dotted with mature chestnuts, beeches and conifers, as well as newly planted specimens. There are three superb *Prunus serrula* showing off their shiny, rich brown bark, a grove of *Betula jacquemontii* with contrasting pale cream trunks, *Araucaria* araucana or the monkey puzzle, and a tall lime tree. The latter obviously varies considerably in form as I have never seen such large seed heads, almost as good as a flowering shrub. The garden does have some herbaceous plants, apricot foxgloves in the shade of trees, as well as ground cover suitable for large areas such as the invasive *Lamium galeobdolon* 'Variegatum' and many spring bulbs — but the trees are the thing, and rightly dominate the scene.

The family in residence have owned the property for many years, but although the present occupants retained the best of the mature trees, the whole garden had to be reorganised when they moved in, as well as

fine crops of nettles and ground elder dealt with. It is now packed with interest, from the well designed iron gates, all individually commissioned to fit their allotted spaces, to the pots of red geraniums on the steps leading up to the imposing front door. This charming homely touch is typical of the attention to detail evident throughout the whole garden.

From the front of the house one sees trees and grass, but a sheltered side looks over a ha-ha towards fields dotted with cows grazing peacefully, more beautiful trees and distant blue hills. I thought the Millennium Avenue of oaks a wonderful way to mark the changing centuries. They are perfectly placed, and approached through another imaginatively designed pair of tall iron gates.

There are many old yews in the garden, some probably older than the house, and as well as making a good dark background also help to shelter other more vulnerable plants. Although the house is 650 feet above sea level, some generally supposed tender subjects such as a *Magnolia grandiflora* and pittosporum thrive close to the house walls. A special delight is the large specimen of *Acer platanoides* 'Drummondii', with its lovely light, variegated foliage set against the deep green of the yews. This tree can very easily revert to plain green, but the specimen at Bitterley is a perfect shape and all variegated. Also in this area, the enormous clipped mounds of foliage and the humps of fastigiate copper beech with almost pink new growth make a perfect contrast with the feathery foliage of larch and cedar. A late summer herbaceous border near the tall gates was packed with valerian, dog daisies and phlox when we visited, all backed by a wall and more ancient yews.

Following a path around the side of the house one comes upon a gate leading to the Norman church, its extraordinary timber-framed spire and lancet windows in full view. It is mostly Early English, but was restored in the late nineteenth-century. Inside is a Norman font and a thirteenth-century coffer, while the graveyard boasts a fine churchyard cross. Rare trees in this part of the garden include *Acer capillipes*, a small snake bark maple from Japan, *Clerodendrum trichotomum*, really a large shrub with unusual bright blue berries, and *Amelanchier lamarckii*, ideal for autumn colour and spring flowers.

Hidden behind hedges and walls is a productive kitchen garden, the vegetables laid out in raised beds, while cutting borders are full of old favourites such as alliums, alstroemeria, eryngiums, roses, sedum and tobacco plants, all interspersed with pillars of sweet peas. Foliage is not forgotten, for

there is artemisia, in a gorgeous grey feathery form, purple cotinus and fennel. Old espalier apples grown tall and loaded with fruit back the main borders, while the lollo-rossa lettuce look almost as colourful as the flowers. The centre piece here is a rose pergola, giving the whole area structure and shape in the winter time.

The fine trees, sweeping lawns and grand house make Bitterley Court a classic land-scape garden, but with warm individual touches that bring it to life and add other dimensions to its beauty.

Bridgwalton House · Morville

A superbly designed plantswoman's garden, full of rare and interesting treasures. Open occasionally for the Historic Churches Trust. Please telephone: 01746 714401 for details

What makes a great garden? Imagination of course, colour sense, knowing your plants, a clear headed idea of what you want, and that little bit of extra flair that makes a garden special. The owner of the garden at Bridgwalton House possesses all of the above, and I think can also legitimately lay claim to the title of artist. It is difficult to find enough superlatives to describe this beautiful garden.

It is about one acre in size on gravelly soil deep in the lush south Shropshire countryside. The house it surrounds is modern and sits in the middle of a long plot, so that there is almost an equal amount of garden to front and rear. It is windy, and with such free draining soil, often dries out in summer.

The garden was begun only nine years ago, the owner finding just grass and a great many weeds on site. Trees planted then are now approaching maturity, making it hard to believe they have been in the ground for such a short time. There are also numerous large shrubs and an outstanding collection of conifers. Lots of the latter were bought with a label stating 'dwarf', but there must be something in the soil, as many are far removed from that description. All the evergreens make a wonderful, unchanging background for the herbaceous perennials, as well as being easy to grow on gravel. An added bonus is that they give the garden structure in the winter, while many can be carefully pruned to fit into their allotted positions.

The owner has had no formal horticultural training and employs no gardener, learning by doing all the hard work herself. The complicated design was worked out on paper, and plant combinations are given much thought before proceeding. Soft colours — blues, mauves, or subtle pinks and reds — are favoured throughout the garden, so that any bright splash such as *Crocosmia* 'Lucifer', really sings out. Not the least of the garden's charms is the imaginative use of stone, all found on site or from nearby fields. These sympathetically weathered pebbles, flat rocks and huge chunks of granite are utilized in raised beds, paving, and focal points throughout the whole area.

The house is approached by a long straight drive, with great clumps of the hardy blue *Agapanthus* 'Bressingham Blue' stealing the show on a hot afternoon in July. To the right of the drive a curving lawn has deep borders of mixed shrubs and herbaceous perennials. Here, I was drawn to a magnificent specimen of that best of all blue spruces, *Picea pungens* 'Thomsen', close to a favourite scabious, *Scabiosa* 'Clive Greaves'. The owner states that this is quite the best form, as not only is the colour marvellous, but it does not need staking.

A gravel section close to the shelter of a garage boasted a tall *Stipa gigantea* in full flower, as well as the variegated *Yucca filamentosa* 'Variegata'. One of these was also in flower, and the combination of airy grass with stiff yucca could surely not be bettered for a hot, dry, well-drained position. My eye was then drawn to a hydrangea perfectly placed against the wall of the house, two gorgeous urns overflowing with fuchsia and geraniums, as well as a stone trough planted with Busy Lizzies in pink and white. Very simple and effective, set off to perfection by the dark green conifer background.

The front garden alone would make Bridgwalton House outstanding, but one slips through a narrow gap in the hedge to be confronted by an even better one. I loved the pond near the terrace. A perfect size for its position, and set with more weathered rocks, as well as quite the most perfect, green, conical conifer that I have ever encountered; I could not believe it wasn't regularly clipped. This is *Picea albertiana* 'Conica', and cannot be too highly recommended for a small garden.

There is a lawn at the back of the house, giving that essential green space on which to rest the eye, but paths lead off in all directions to a hexagonal summer house, flower beds and more shrub and mixed borders. The beautiful foliage of the rare cut leaf form of birch, *Betula pendula* 'Dalecarlica', as well as many other well chosen trees overhead. There is a pergola on one side of the lawn with clematis and vines, while rounding every corner one meets with a treasure. The pure white form of *Lavatera arborea* for example, an absolute terror to get going — the owner states that it is cut down every year in the winter but always comes back. I wish mine did. Then the variegated *Daphne x burkwoodii* 'Variegata' and *Hebe armstrongii*, the

latter now rarely seen, and an absolutely unique bronze colour. I must also mention the extraordinary long vista stretching right down the side of the plot, with a corn field as one border and the garden proper on the other. Once again packed with unusual plants and ending with a mirror to extend the illusion of space.

A white gate under a bamboo arch at the end of the garden leads one to expect something special, and you are not disappointed. This is the new Japanese garden, recently planted and not yet mature, but already a joy to walk around and showing the same flair encountered in the rest of the plot. A dry river has been constructed, the 'water', made of blue-grey slate, as well as stone bridges, raised beds and a restrained use of ornamental Japanese lanterns. The planting scheme is mostly blue, with grasses, massed *Iris pallida* 'Variegata', and again lots of dwarf conifers. My special favourites here are a dwarf golden cedar and the bamboo *Phyllostachys nigra*, with jet black stems.

The Japanese garden is typical of the plot as a whole, full of wonderfully astute touches such as the flat staddle stones planted with sempervirums, only noticed when leaving. Truly a garden to enchant.

Brockton Court • Brockton

A large country garden with herbaceous beds, shrubs, good trees and a fascinating new water feature. Open under the National Gardens Scheme, see Yellow Book

Brockton Court once functioned as a working farm, with nothing in the garden of value save some mature trees — a magnificent cedar, three gigantic copper beeches and an avenue of elms. The avenue succumbed to Dutch elm disease and only one copper beech and the cedar remain, but the garden proper has expanded over the past twelve years into a highly original, yet typical, English country garden.

The area close to the house, which includes the original farm garden, is laid out with smooth lawns and borders filled with roses and annuals, the whole dominated by the great cedar, and the beautiful, mellow brick and red sandstone house. The main building was constructed in 1678, but a black and white timber wing had to be demolished when the owners moved in over forty years ago. Parts of the house are believed to have been a courthouse with ties to the priory at Much Wenlock, and this is given further credence by the remains of an ancient chapel in an adjoining meadow. The house has a stately, symmetrical air for such an old building, with a brick and sandstone porch projecting into the entrance drive adding to the character of the front garden.

The old farmhouse plot in the front of the house was once divided from the fields around by a ha-ha, but this has been filled in and a new garden designed. Visitors walk through a mini arboretum planted up with the common native oaks, the unusual tulip trees and the rare alder, *Alnus glutinosa* 'Imperialis' — to reach a newly constructed cascade and pond. The pond and arboretum have been in existence for some time, but because of the steep slope from trees to water, it proved to be the perfect site for a dramatic cascade falling over several levels of Grinshill sandstone to the enlarged pond at the base. This part of the garden has still to mature, and there have been some problems with blanket weed, but the whole concept fits the site to perfection, and further plantings are envisaged for the future.

The main garden lies to the side of the house and is approached under an iron pergola with high hedges on either side. One passes an enclosed swimming pool on the right, its sheltering walls hung with roses, then into a large, oblong, open space which seems to encompass every feature found in the archetypal English country garden. I loved the way everything came together with no divisions, the vegetables and fruit close to the high walls exquisitely laid out in neat rows; strawberries next to tall climbers — including the difficult *Rosa banksiae alba*; island beds of mixed shrubs and perennials; or a utilitarian greenhouse close to a dignified sandstone sundial. Best of all, an old orchard of gnarled, dwarf, fruit trees in closely cropped grass, a Judas tree making a spectacular centrepiece.

This part of the garden was not designed on paper, it just grew, but an artist's eye is detectable in the colour juxtapositions of iris, roses, dianthus and peonies. I admired the composition of tall foxtail lilies — eremurus — together with rounded clumps of lavender; but my favourite 'flower bed' turned out to be a small pond almost completely hidden by *Iris laevigata* and a wonderful clump of the Japanese iris, — *I. kaempferi* — in rich mauve. This was backed by shrubs such as ceanothus, hamamelis, *Buddleia alternifolia* and small trees like prostrate cedar and *Acer dissectum*. It is extraordinary that ceanothus were once considered too tender to grow outdoors in this country, and recommended as a warm wall or conservatory shrub in some old gardening books.

The soil throughout the garden is heavy clay, which usually comes to light when new areas are worked, though the garden close to the house has been under cultivation for so many years it is now a pleasure to deal with and resembles fertile loam. A conservatory juts out from the house and creates a sitting out place, with a sunken garden full of colourful, overflowing pots. This is an ideal spot from which to admire the fruit, vegetables and flowers growing harmoniously within the sheltering walls.

Burford House Gardens • Tenbury Wells

An elegant Georgian house dating from 1728, surrounded by extensive gardens featuring island beds and the National Clematis Collection. Open frequently in season.

Please telephone: 01584 810777 for details

The gardens, house and nursery at Burford have seen a change of ownership and some expansion since they were included in our first book on Shropshire gardens fourteen years ago. Situated right on the border between Shropshire and Herefordshire, they run alongside the River Teme, and now include a further area of wild meadow across a rustic, grassed bridge.

There has been a dwelling at Burford since mediaeval times, but the ruined castle which once occupied the site was almost totally demolished in the eighteenth century, and a distinguished, symmetrical, red brick house constructed, incorporating some foundations from the old building. It was further extended in Victorian times, and became a large private house. After another metamorphosis into a school, it, together with eleven acres of land, was purchased by John Treasure and his brothers in 1954. They demolished the Victorian additions (excepting the stable block) began to develop the world famous clematis nursery, and are largely responsible for the layout of the gardens as one sees them today.

Burford House Gardens cover roughly four acres, and are situated chiefly to the rear and one side of the main building — though the house can be viewed from the front in all its Georgian elegance. Visitors look across wide lawns and a long canal both echoing the formality and simplicity of the slightly austere, square building. After passing through the house and out into the garden proper, however, the atmosphere could not be more different. Burford was envisaged at the height of the fashion for island beds, and is a perfect example of this important and

influential style, though there are many more sides to this wonderful garden.

I had forgotten quite what a good collection of trees exist at Burford. Now, after fifty years or more, most are at the height of their beauty, and include a huge specimen of *Betula* 'Hergest' with glorious bark, surrounded by a blue-grey iron circular seat, as well as *Robinia pseudoacacia* 'Frisia' close to the river, a glowing bright yellow in the summer sunshine. Other notables are a southern beech, *Nothofagus antarctica*, an extraordinary Douglas fir reaching up to the heavens, as well as a comprehensive collection of acers for autumn colour and cherries for spring blossom.

There are wide borders following the walls filled with interesting herbaceous perennials and shrubs, all planted with a sophisticated eye for colour co-ordination. I loved the pink penstemons and the blue-grey perovskia together with rich blue salvias and

Clematis Florida Alba Plena

agapanthus. Also a delight is the campanula bed in blue and white from massed plantings of *Campanula alliariifolia* and *C. latifolia*, just a touch of mauvey-pink coming from *C. lactiflora* 'Loddon Anna'.

The white lantern of the stable block and the church tower are visible over the wall in this part of the garden, forming an impressive back-drop to a large circular pond covered in water lilies, and a sheltered corner garden containing some tender foliage plants such as pittosporum, phormium and *Fatsia japonica*. Here also, a superb dark blue deciduous ceanothus is set off by self-seeding Scotch thistles, the silver leaf pear, and lamb's ears, all in grey; a covered seat painted in pale cream placed to take full advantage of the scent from Madonna lilies. Nearby is a sunken pond with a lead heron, leading to a ditch garden filled with arum lilies and filipendula. The background here includes a Judas tree, while in another direction the eye is led over astrantia, iris and astilbe to a bank of white hydrangea. There is also a 'hot' border backed by purple foliage containing *Crocosmia* 'Lucifer', some tall cardoons, and *Dahlia* 'Bishop of Landaff'. I very much approved of the way seed heads are allowed to stay, with poppies and foxtail lilies providing perhaps the best examples in early July. Grasses are also a feature close to the river, and make good partners for the graceful *Dierama pulcherrimum*, or angel's fishing rods, as does the bamboo, which grows large and lush in the damp shade.

One cannot visit Burford without some reference to the wonderful collection of clematis in evidence throughout the garden. Most are grown informally over shrubs and walls, while others tumble out of urns, or wind through heathers on a steep bank. My favourite combination is *Clematis orientalis* 'Bill Mackenzie' in partnership with a large philadelphus or orange blossom, the white and yellow flowers together against a deep blue sky providing an unforgettable picture.

A completely fresh venture instigated by the new owner of Burford is a wild flower meadow also planned as a sculpture garden partially supported by the Arts Council of Great Britain, and curating exhibitions of the highest quality. The layout is perfect, with various hedged alcoves for the sculptures set against a background of trees. When we visited the whole area was a sea of yellow from the corn marigold, with groups of corn cockle (now very rare in the wild) and dog daisies. The idea is to offer visitors modern, contemporary sculpture in a natural setting. Altogether an exciting and imaginative venture which sets the seal on a truly lovely garden.

The Citadel · Weston-Under-Redcastle

An extraordinary castellated house in four acres of unique gardens surrounding a sandstone outcrop.

Open under the National Gardens Scheme, see Yellow Book

The Citadel is a miniature, red sandstone castle, on a sandstone bluff overlooking the Shropshire plains in one direction and the Welsh hills in another. It is close to Hawkstone Park, the only Grade 1 listed landscape in Shropshire, with its world renowned collection of follies, grottoes and hidden pathways. In fact, The Citadel was built in the 1820s (*c.*1790 according to Pevsner) as a dower house, by a descendant of the same Sir Roland Hill who created the great park with all its eccentricities. With such a history, one would expect The Citadel to be different, but I think that it can truly claim to be unique, taking the form of three large turrets with castellated joining walls like a mediaeval fortress. The three turrets are the coat of arms of the Hill family neatly incorporated into the design of the house.

The gardens cover four acres, and the original layout is believed to have been designed by yet another Hill, this time the Rev. John Hill. The owner's father purchased the house and grounds in the 1950s, when the gardens had been very much neglected, but a gradual programme of work has restored them to their former glory. A delightful summer house, for example, with a breathtaking — if windy — view of the Welsh hills, has been sympathetically reconstructed on its original stone floor, the owners taking immense care to recreate the early Victorian picturesque, 'rustic look' correctly. Red sandstone for any repairs to the house has to come from Scotland, Grinshill stone, quarried locally, being pinkish-grey in colour.

The glories of the garden are the trees — including one of the most imposing copper beeches that I have ever seen — the rhododendrons and azaleas, once consisting mostly of the common mauve form *R. ponticum* but now augmented by many different varieties; and the great sandstone outcrop in the centre of the garden. The latter is laced by meandering paths, a grove of acers recently planted, as well as many beautiful and impressive large trees. The paths are mulched with pine needles and chipped tree bark, but the sandstone bones of the great outcrop are never far from the surface, often breaking through and creating what I can only describe as a very large, natural, rock garden. The acer grove is still young, but beautifully placed where it is sheltered from winds and early frosts by more mature trees, the whole under-planted with Spanish bluebells. These flowers have had something of a bad press lately, as they are unscented and tend to overpower our native English bluebells when planted close together. They are vigorous and easy to grow, however, and in the right place, such as at The Citadel, can look wonderful in mature woodland.

A path around the central outcrop bordered by hedges, allows occasional glimpses of the glorious views and leads to the more formal summer garden at the rear of the house. I admired the border of laburnum trees under-planted with lavender, a mauvey-blue ribbon marking the edge of the lawn and leading one on to the vegetable garden. This is laid out in cottage style, the vegetables interspersed with flowers.

Close by is a delightful and quite separate walled garden that has variously been a rose garden and a vineyard. The latter once contained an experimental range of

German grapes but was not a huge success although some white wine was produced. Now glorious lilies and cistus bushes with white flowers fill the beds, while tender climbers such as *Solanum crispum* and the yellow *Fremontodendron* 'California Glory' clothe the high walls around a central lawn. The entrance pillars to this garden are particularly fine, topped by stone baskets.

The rear of The Citadel comes as something of a surprise as it is built of brick, although the same muted red as the sandstone front. Here the garden is paved and laid out with raised beds, a pond and a pergola. Many pots give the whole area a formal feel, while architectural plants such as phormium, clipped hollies and hebes, suit the orderly surroundings. Once again all is in keeping with the ambience of the house, even the outdoor table being a large circular piece of red sandstone with a matching support.

A walk around this garden is a revealing experience, as it incorporates everything that makes a garden special — trees, flowers, views, as well as the fascinating historical context which gives it that unique and original flavour.

1 Cross Villas • Ruyton XI Towns

A small village garden full of ideas, and with an impressive collection of clematis.

Open under the National Gardens Scheme, see Yellow Book

If I made a list of all the plants at 1 Cross Villas, over forty clematis and sixty-four rose varieties alone, you would imagine a garden of at least an acre. Now picture the same number of plants in a plot about an eighth that size, and you will get some idea of the overflowing abundance throughout the garden.

The house, which sits close to the road, used to be the old village Post Office, and is a typical late Victorian/Edwardian 'villa', in red brick. It once had a much larger garden, part of which still belongs to the house and is accessed by a right of way past the old privy into what was once the laundry 'drying green'. It is in effect a split site, the part furthest away from the main garden boasting a tiny, semicircular lawn, and as overflowing with plants as the rest of the plot. Even the fish in the raised pond increase at breakneck

speed, the owner informing me that numbers have grown from eleven to about forty in just two years. Needless to say I asked about fertilizer for such a plethora of well grown plants so closely packed, and was assured that a little horse manure somehow squeezed in every two years is all the food they get.

When we visited in early July, the roses were waning, but the superb collection of viticella clematis were just coming into their own. The viticella group are among the smallest of the clematis family, though can be vigorous in growth. They have fewer sepals than the larger flowered hybrids, delightful nodding heads — on many varieties turned back like the Turk's cap lily — and long stalks which hold them away from the foliage so that you can see each individual bloom. At 1 Cross Villas, every wall,

wooden trellis, arch, climbing rose and the house plays host to these delicate plants, with yet more growing in pots or tumbling out of raised beds. Where I would have hesitated to plant one, the owner has put in two or three, all scrambling through one another to reach the light, and blooming profusely *en route*.

Gardening started in earnest about sixteen years ago, the plot then containing a rowan tree, some elders, a patch of rhubarb, and a great deal of ground elder. Fortunately the ground at 1 Cross Villas is sandy, so that weeds do come up easily, and the owners find that the best way to deal with persistent perennial offenders like ground elder, is simply to keep at it and never give up. Most of the narrow winding paths in the garden are of gravel, and were once much wider, but as self-sown seedlings encroached, they became narrower. I too have found that many plants such as campanulas, hardy geranium and euphorbia, seed well into gravel, providing a good source of free plants.

The front garden is truly minute and has been recently revamped, but the eye is drawn immediately to the three clematis over the front door, all flowering together: 'Arabella' in pale blue, and 'Etoile Rose', as its name suggests, in pink, to the right is the elegant 'Alba Luxurians', a universal favourite with early flowers almost entirely green, later ones being white with green tips, while some are pure white. Also in the front garden, is *C. viticella* 'Purpurea Plena Elegans', by a strange coincidence, growing in the identical way that I have mine on a small obelisk. This is a charming double, with small rosettes of flattened sepals in rich purple. At the back of the house is another form of similar shape, but in colour, a glorious dark blue.

Herbaceous perennials are not neglected, in spite of the lack of space; the muted blues, mauves and reds of the clematis set off by the salmon pinks of a stand of *Alstroemeria* ligtu hybrids, and a lovely pale yellow

Anthemis tinctoria, called appropriately 'Sauce Hollandaise'. There is just room in the garden for several sitting out places, all needless to say overhung with climbers. But I am sure sure that the danger of an occasional spider down the neck is compensated for by the scent of the roses.

A look over the wall at 1 Cross Villas, or better still a stroll around the whole garden, is an amazing experience, showing just what can be achieved in a small garden if you have the courage to go along with your big ideas.

Cruckfield House • Ford

An outstanding four acre garden with extensive lake, unusual herbaceous plants, trees, shrubs and ornamental kitchen garden. Open under the National Gardens Scheme, see Yellow Book

It is hard to find words adequate to describe the wonderful garden which surrounds Cruckfield House, though the idea that something special lies beyond the iron gates leading into the garden proper is hinted at by the line of ancient limes bordering the entrance drive, their gnarled grey trunks indicating great age. A house has existed on the same spot since Jacobean times — parts are still visible at the rear — but the front is Georgian and the wings Victorian, the present owners having added a garden room.

This is a garden of vistas, and a classic picture is immediately opened up on the left as one approaches the house. A large lake becomes a reflecting mirror for a Grecian temple in pale grey stone perfectly placed at the far end. Closer inspection reveals *Iris sibirica* in many shades of blue, as well as other moisture loving plants. The lake is large enough to accommodate big shrubs such as willow, juniper and cornus at its edges without being swamped, mostly chosen for their beautiful leaves and autumn colour. Water lilies in pink and cream cover the lake, but not in such profusion as to destroy the reflections. It is a haven for wildlife, with kingfishers and herons often sighted.

Such a large stretch of water is some-times difficult to tie into a landscape, but at Cruckfield the ideal solution arrived at is to mow paths around through wild meadow grass full of dog daisies and buttercups. These paths are meticulously maintained, as is the whole garden; not an easy task, as the owners garden completely organically, eschewing all insecticides, pesticides and weed-killers.

The temple is backed by many specimen trees, notably larches — in their sharpest spring green when we visited. Others sited in the long, flower bespeckled grass, are a grove of the white barked *Betula jacquemontii* with dazzling trunks, *Cedrus deodara*, *Prunus serrula*, a great favourite with its polished red-brown bark, and eucalyptus.

The owners of Cruckfield House moved into the area twenty-four years ago, finding just a small flower garden at the front and a vegetable plot at the rear, with extensive lawns and grassland. Over those years it has become almost a full time occupation and gradually extended to cover four acres.

The lake alone makes the garden special, but a second superb vista meets the eye from either end of the rose and peony walk. This narrow garden, bordered by hornbeam hedges, leads to the side of the house and a small courtyard garden where a fountain in a formal pool plays. *En route* visitors pass an armillary sphere at a cross vista back to the lake, walk through a beautiful old building that was once a stable, and past another small, brick paved area with terracotta pots and warm pink stone walls.

All the pots and sculpture in the garden are sympathetically placed to make the most of their setting. A giant empty pot on its side near the lake, for example, provides a good contrast with the 'live' green sculpture of a gunnera. Then I realised that from the long walk it was just visible again across the lake, thus giving two entrancing viewpoints.

Peonies and roses come and go very quickly (perhaps this is part of their charm) so the owners of Cruckfield House have added iris, delphiniums and lupins in the long walk to extend the season. All my favourite shrub roses are represented: 'William Lobb' — sometimes known as Old Velvet Moss — with its habit of fading from crimson to violet; 'Rosa Mundi', the best striped rose and a lovely scent; as well as the rarely planted 'White Grootendorse', with pretty pale flowers, their edges serrated as if cut with a scissors.

Lilies are mostly confined to pots in the paved garden, though I noted a spike of *Lilium Cardiocrinum giganteum* in full flower at the back of the border. Even the wood store is a work of art, beautifully stacked and hidden behind 'flower gates', obviously especially commissioned from an artist to exactly complement their position.

The vegetable garden is small, neatly laid out with brick paths, and hidden from sight by high walls and hedges. Passing through it to the side of the house, one enters the formal garden viewed from afar with its pond and fountain. As the slope is steep, it has been terraced with local stone, tables and chairs indicating that it is a pleasant, sheltered sun spot for eating out.

There is still more to see, with a third, clearly defined garden sited on the south side of the house. Here gravel marks the way and provides space for low growing plants to overhang the path. These lead you hither and thither with no particular pattern, and pass huge clumps of hardy geranium, silver leafed plants such as ballota and senecio, as well as more shrub roses for height, and a

magnificent *Cornus controversa* 'Variegata', with sweeping, horizontal branches. Hedges here are holly and yew, sheltering the area well, as the tender *Cytisus battandieri* and pittosporum are thriving, while a Japanese acer shades a garden seat.

A pond is the centre of a green oasis of ferns and conifers. At its side is perhaps my favourite piece of sculpture in the whole garden — one of David Goode's exquisitely wicked looking goblins. This one drinks water from a bronze leaf and stands in a drift of *Alchemilla mollis*. David Goode calls it 'The Drinker'.

Every corner of this garden reflects its makers' empathy with the plants, landscape, sculpture and setting. Nothing is out of place, nothing jars. A real labour of love.

Cruckmeole House • Near Shrewsbury

A large plantsman's garden, home to the National Collections of convallarias and rosoeas.

Open occasionally for the Historic Churches Trust. Please telephone: 01743 860295 for details

The owners of Cruckmeole House were founder members of the Shropshire branch of the National Council for the Conservation of Plants and Gardens (N.C.C.P.G.) and hold two National Collections of unusual plants. I can only say that it shows, for this is a plantsman's garden *par excellence*. The setting, deep in the Shropshire countryside, is superb, the gardens — four acres bordered by the River Rea — magical. The house, dating from Tudor times but with remakes in 1775 and 1835, is an absolute gem; but it is the plants that draw the eye, from majestic trees to herbaceous borders overflowing with the rare and the choice.

The soil in the garden is basically a neutral loam, but in typical Shropshire fashion it does vary even within four acres, giving the owners of Cruckmeole House a range of conditions to suit many types of plant. They also have the advantage of light woodland bordering their property, an ideal situation for many bulbs, a river for moisture loving perennials — though occasional floods make this a chancy operation — also open mixed borders in full sun, and a plethora of walls for climbers and tender subjects. I loved the varied collection of hosta — sometimes liable to slug damage in the open garden — grown in pots and gathered into one dramatic group in a shady corner.

The owners also keep part of their National Collections potted up, as well as growing them in the open — just in case. Convallaria, better known as lily-of-the-valley, are fairly easy to grow once they get going, but the rosoeas' fleshy roots demand deep planting in well drained soil, preferably with plenty of leaf mould added. Their delicate purple or yellow flowers can light up a shady corner, however, and are well worth the trouble.

In the main garden I admired the way the death of an enormous larch, which once dominated the wide sweeping lawn to the side of the house, had been turned from a tragedy into an opportunity. Its replacement is a cedar surrounded by a variety of the shrub rose moyesii, all chosen for autumn hips as well as summer flowers.

Another lovely rose, looking its best against a dark background of yews, is the single white *Rosa* 'Wickwar'. It has orange-yellow stamens and the most unusual greyish foliage, the semi-shade seeming to bring out its simple beauty. Also in this area is a purple hardy geranium with a black blotch called 'Ivan'. It is very like the more common psilostemon, but a much darker colour and also appears to glow in the shade of the border.

Cruckmeole House has a very large garden by any standards and it was wonderful to see a huge *Juniperus x media* 'Pfitzerana', really given its head and allowed to spread. This architectural conifer is ruined if one constantly prunes it back, but could soon cover an entire small garden if left to its own devices. Similarly in another part of the garden, great spiraeas tower overhead. To gardeners used to seeing tiny, neat bushes grown in endless front gardens, *S. veitchii* and *S. canescans* in full flower can come as something of a shock, but a pleasant one.

So many of the plants were completely new to me that a visit to Cruckmeole is something of a botanic lesson, from *Bursaria spinosa* on the house wall, one of the first plants grown by the owners for the N.C.C.P.G., to a *Buddleia lindleyana*, its bright green leaves like no other of the species I have ever come across. Helpfully, most of the rarer plants are named with small unobtrusive plant labels, the owners admitting that it helps them to remember too!

Do not think that the common is despised at Cruckmeole, as one of the owners is a flower arranger who grows most of her own material. Old favourites of mine included *Geranium orientalitibeticum*, a clear mauve form with the most delightful variegated foliage; the everlasting pea, *Lathyrus latifolius*, in both pink and white — unfortunately they have no scent — to a beautiful *Hydrangea paniculata*, green in bud, but pure white when fully open; which, I was informed, was grown from seed.

Roses abound throughout the garden, on pillars, walls and as part of mixed herbaceous and shrub beds, not to mention a huge specimen of *Rosa* 'Leontine Gervais', covering the entire stable wall. There was once an old rose garden, but as the ground became 'rose sick' it was metamorphosed into herbaceous beds, and the roses became part of the overall garden picture.

It is hard to pick a favourite plant, but I must mention *Fabiana imbricata*; a little like a tree heather at first glance, but smothered in what can only be described as tiny, pale mauve-blue tubes. Then there are the foxgloves. The gorgeous *Digitalis lutea*, with pale, straw coloured miniature 'gloves'; the brown foxglove *D. ferruginea*, as lovely in bud — a green sculpture — as in flower, and *D. laevigata*, a unique burnt-orange colour.

Among the trees a yellow magnolia, called appropriately 'Yellow River', is an especially choice new addition, as well as many newly planted hamamelis and a mature *Acer griseum*, with its tattered red-brown bark. The owners informed me that the latter is an excellent weather predictor, as it never breaks its buds until the last frost of winter is past.

Cruckmeole House is an enthusiast's garden in every sense of the word. But who would not be enthusiastic in such a setting and with such a plant collection.

David Austin Roses • Albrighton

The place to see roses (900 varieties) especially the unique English Roses bred by David Austin.

Open daily in season. Please telephone: 01902 376376 for details

David Austin Roses is a commercial nursery well known as breeders of the world famous English roses and what are generally called shrub roses. But the vast collection which can be viewed in the show gardens encompass not only these but every other form that one can think of, including old roses species, hybrid teas and climbing roses. It must now be one of the very best places in the country to see roses in all their glory, laid out in an extensive garden well designed to show off this popular plant, whether as climbers, ramblers, bush, or ground-cover. I must emphasise that these are not nursery beds, but a true garden — or series of gardens — which, with its high hedges of well clipped *Cupressus leylandii*, totally isolates one from the more commercial aspects of the site, and gives the overall impression of a private garden around a house.

Much development has taken place since we visited the garden for our first book on Shropshire gardens, though the sight and scent of the garden in high summer was always a sensual knockout. The circular garden of English roses has matured, the box hedging echoing the design of an Elizabethan knot garden filled with roses instead of coloured gravel, a stone figure a perfect centre piece. Here, the golden-yellow rose 'Graham Thomas', one of the most popular of the English variety, is an especial favourite of mine with its healthy green foliage and delightful fragrance. English roses were developed by Mr. Austin to combine the beauty and scent of the old roses, such as gallicas, damasks and Chinas, with the hardyness and repeat flowering performance of the hybrid teas. The many superb varieties now available in every colour and which are on view in the gardens are a triumph of plant breeding, and deservedly very popular.

A new garden, again enclosed by high hedges, sports a long central canal edged with bush roses, while a covered pavilion, ideal for sitting and admiring, makes a visual

full stop at one end. I was intrigued to see the benches under the red tiled roof backed by the English rose, 'Jayne Austin', a glorious creamy-apricot, its tea rose scent intensified by the surrounding roof and walls.

All smaller gardens lead off from a long walk which is covered from end to end by a series of pergolas and brick columns ideal for displaying the climbers and ramblers, whilst old roses, modern shrub and English forms, fill the beds below.

Perhaps my favourite area is the species garden at the end of the long, paved walk, which contains all the more delicate pimpinellifolia, wild roses and their hybrid variants. Most of these extend the rose season by exhibiting colourful hips as well as flowers. Others, especially *Rosa glauca*, also boast the most beautiful blue-grey foliage, and will even come true from seed.

It is difficult to pick just a selection of roses to describe from the many on show, but an unusual bush which caught my eye was 'Rhapsody in Blue', a modern shrub rose in a quite incredible shade of lavender, and which I am sure will be of great interest to flower arrangers. The sounds of bees buzzing led us to the pimpinellifolia roses, 'Robbie Burns', a single pink, 'Falkland', a tight, pale-pink double, and the glowing crimson, 'William III'. All the latter have good large hips in the autumn, and the delightful, neat, characteristic foliage.

Coming out of the species rose garden, I noted the old climber 'Maigold', as its name suggests, a shining warm yellow, as well as a new, repeat flowering rambler, 'Malvern Hills'. This has coppery-yellow flowers a shade lighter than 'Maigold', but appears equally vigorous and trouble free.

Finally, I must mention the many interesting sculptures in the garden by Pat Austin, used as focal points or centre pieces and all depicting in some way the flower to which the garden is dedicated, either as posy, garland or rosette.

The Canal Garden

The Dower House, Morville Hall • Bridgnorth

A one-and-a-half-acre garden in the grounds of Morville Hall designed in various historical styles.

Open from the beginning of April to the end of September, Sundays, Wednesdays and

Bank Holiday Mondays, 2–6 p.m. but please telephone: 01746 714407 to check details

Morville Hall itself is a Grade 1 listed building owned by the National Trust and sited close to a superb Norman church which began life as a Benedictine priory. Built of grey stone, the imposing Elizabethan house was much altered in the eighteenth century, and is also surrounded by an attractive period garden and small vineyard.

A visit to the Dower House is a journey back in time, showing gardening as history. Its creator is a garden historian and writer who set out in 1988 to reflect the story of the house and the people who lived in it through the surrounding plot. This is one of the few gardens visited for this book that had been consciously 'designed', as the National Trust required detailed plans. Its owner had never made a garden before, but had an overwhelming interest in, as well as access to, a wealth of books and manuals for research. She then began, making a journey not only back in time, but from the theoretical to the practical.

All that remained of the original Dower House grounds when the National Trust took over the property in the 1960s was a large pear tree — a seventeenth-century German variety called 'Forelle' — and a rough orchard. The designer of the gardens as they appear today realised that she would have to go right back to basics, and a bull-dozer was brought in to level the ground; she then had the whole area grassed before the outline of the plan on paper was marked out in a series of yew hedges. The latter were only nine inches high when planted, but are now all a uniform seven feet six inches, and divide the garden into many separate areas,

each reflecting a chapter in the house's past and telling the story of English gardening in the style of different historical periods. The whole area covers only one and a half acres, but appears much larger, as one wanders from one enclosed plot to another, the whole surrounded by mature trees and distant fields.

The first plot, close to the house, reflects its Elizabethan origins and contains a knot garden complete with boards to retain the great banks of lavender outlining them. Other boarded beds hold apple trees, while a cherry, heavy with immature fruit when we visited, decorates the front of the house.

I loved the contrast of purple lavender with the grey stone of the house, and it is worth noting here that each partitioned garden contains only plants which were grown in this country at the time of that particular garden's origin.

The main plan of the garden revolves around a turf maze, which makes a simple, restful, all green circle after the vibrant colour of the Victorian Rose Border. The centrepiece of the Maze Garden — which consists not of hedges but raised grass — is a disease resistant elm bred in the U.S.A., hopefully the first of many, and marking a resurgence of the elm in this country.

When we visited in late June, The Dower House shrub roses — which are a speciality of the garden — were spilling over borders and paths, their scent filling the air; each group, in rich reds, pinks, and creamy/white, punctuated by self-sown foxgloves. Grey notes came from *Eryngium giganteum*, which also seeds in the most accommodating way, and tall cardoons at the back of the border.

The Canal Garden is a total contrast to the Victorian Rose Border's exuberance, being a formal, restrained water feature with stiff box hedging, standard trees in pale, grey-blue Versailles tubs, and severely clipped hollies.

The Ornamental Fruit and Vegetable Garden is bisected by an apple tunnel as well as a separate pear tunnel, which provides space to grow many old and curious varieties. In the vegetable garden proper, however, useable quantities of modern origin are grown, including basics like potatoes, while the corners boast huge clumps of rhubarb, currant bushes, or fruit trees underplanted with strawberries. The ornamental element comes from the billowing white roses planted between the cordoned apples and pears, so that all the senses are catered for as one walks through.

The Cloister Garden reflects the earliest mediaeval period of the grounds, when they

contained a Benedictine Abbey. Here the double row of yew hedges are planted close together, the plan being that they will eventually meet overhead in an arcade. There are openings at the side like the nave of a church, with clipped yews as pillars.

I admired the way the gardens are planned for maximum contrast, the formality of the Cloister Garden emphasised by the Wild Garden nearby. This is part of the old orchard and is now home to nut trees interspersed with cool paths winding amongst species roses and full of hidden birds in full song. The Wild Garden is where the garden proper meets the Shropshire countryside, via an iris border. The other three sides are bounded by a snowdrop walk, a plum walk and the elegant front of the house.

A visit to The Dower House really is a stroll through history, and many people come not only to admire, but to learn something about our gardening past.

Dudmaston · Quatt

A fine, seventeenth-century house, set in eight acres of parkland, with lake, rhododendrons and magnificent trees. Owned by the National Trust and open frequently in season.

Please telephone 01746 780866 for details

There has been a house at Dudmaston since the twelfth century, and a Tudor building is believed to have preceded the present mansion which was begun in the late seventeenth century. Much rebuilding, mostly instigated by the then owner, William Wolryche Whitmore M.P., was carried out in the early nineteenth century, and the 1960s saw a further rationalisation of the main house. Now, however, the house, estate and gardens are in the care of the National Trust and sit serenely in a classic English landscape of trees, meadows and lake.

The garden front faces south overlooking a magnificent stretch of water, with views to the Clee Hills. It looks natural, but was in fact created in 1777 by William Emes, a landscape designer in the style of Repton, who combined several small pools into one large stretch of water known as the Big Pool. The tiny stream which feeds the main lake runs through an intriguing part of the garden called The Dingle. This is a picturesque woodland of walks, seats and cascades

devised in the nineteenth century by one of the ladies of the house and the then head gardener, the appropriately named Walter Wood. It has been recently restored by the National Trust, and is an important survival of this style of landscape design.

When William Wolryche Whitmore owned the property, he ordered the construction of the terraces between the house and the lake, as well as the American border which contains, apart from a wealth of hybrid rhododendrons, many other interesting plants native to the U.S.A. It is this part of the garden which seems to have seen most alteration since our previous visit to Dudmaston. Then, the shrubs had been devastated by the severe winters of the 1980s, much of the American border losing almost all of its mature, original planting. It looked bare and new, but now, after a succession of milder seasons and nearly fifteen years, is approaching its earlier magnificence.

Perhaps the outstanding plant is a large, multi-stemmed, snowdrop tree, *Halesia carolina*, covered in white blossom when we saw it, and under-planted with a drift of English bluebells. It is in a glade of its own, but surrounded by colourful rhododendrons in pinks, creams, mauves and purples, all toned down by the background of green from native oaks, ash and copper beech. Azaleas, the common yellow and a glorious apricot, add both colour and scent, while great groups of hosta with green, yellow and cream variegations, together with more bluebells and the late daffodil *Narcissus poeticus* 'Pheasant Eye', are an inspired under-planting. I suspect the rhododendrons and azaleas were once grouped in island beds, but have now outgrown their allotted spaces to make glades and winding paths which owe more to nature than artifice.

There are a number of well defined island beds further down the hillside, some of mixed shrubs such as magnolias, shrub roses and *Buddleia alternifolia*, but one composed entirely of philadelphus, or orange blossom, including the yellow leaf form, *P. coronarius* 'Aureus'; quite as good for scent as its green leafed cousins. Another is devoted to *Viburnum plicatum* 'Mariesii', its tiered, horizontal habit of growth demanding plenty of room to spread and show off. Further down the hill, close to the lake, a new bog garden is being created with an already mature gunnera surrounded by a planting of mixed filipendula.

Two mighty cedars of Lebanon dominate the lawn in front of the house, but there is also a large *Metasequoia glyptostroboides*, one of the first to be planted in this country, while the park contains specimens of ancient oaks which must be many hundreds of years old.

A rocky sandstone outcrop at the side of the lake has been carefully planted with small shrubs and herbaceous perennials which enjoy good drainage. The aspect and ground conditions obviously suit them, as the cistus, brooms and lavenders have reached an enormous size and spread. Also doing well are the rock roses, phlomis and santolina, which like the same conditions. Low beds of heather at the top of the bank provide winter interest, while lines of roses give scent and colour close to the house without obscuring the wonderful view.

There are many important sculptures in the garden and house, including works by Henry Moore and Barbara Hepworth, the open landscape near the lake lending itself well to the placing of large, semi-abstract pieces.

The main garden revolves around the lake, house and the trees, but it is the details that remain in the memory. The avenue of miniature roses and Welsh poppies on the way to the garden, or the simple, self-sown erigerons in the formal steps leading to the great house.

Field House • Clee St Margaret

A large country garden created for year round interest.

Open under the National Gardens Scheme, see Yellow Book

Field House lies at the centre of a spider's web of narrow lanes in the depths of the beautiful south Shropshire countryside. En route, high hedges studded with elder flowers and dog roses almost meet overhead, occasional gaps revealing breathtaking views in every shade of blue, purple and green over miles of hills and fields. In a garden like Field House — at the top of a hill and with such a setting — one has to make a vital early choice between views and shelter. The owners have wisely opted for good thick wind breaks, including a tall yew hedge and many strategically placed trees.

When they came to the house in 1986, the garden contained a great many conifers. Ninety per cent were grubbed up immediately and replaced by more interesting varieties, as well as choice deciduous trees and large shrubs. These form the basis of the one acre under cultivation and are a great framework to build on, creating what I can only describe as a sophisticated cottage garden. Throughout the entire area, the choice grows alongside the unexceptional. *Picea orientalis* 'Aurea' with its creamy-yellow new growth contrasted with the common larch; astrantia in every shade, from the new and hard to find 'Hadspen Blood', growing cheek-by-jowl with the ordinary kind; *Prunus serrula*, a wonderful specimen with shiny polished bark and the silver birch, almost a weed in some gardens. Everything jostling together in gorgeous disarray, overflowing their allotted positions and self-seeding in every crack and crevice. I can honestly say that I have never seen such well grown, healthy herbaceous perennials planted so closely.

The early nineteenth-century house that the garden surrounds is built of local sandstone and has been much extended over the years. It is an ideal background for climbing plants and is almost hidden from view by a golden hop, purple *Solanum crispum*; *Clematis chrysocoma* — like a white montana — a pale pink rose, a huge *Garrya elliptica*, *Hydrangea petiolaris*, euonymus, and a white rose — and that's just the front! At the side, a complete new wing has been built, the owners being lucky enough to find material that exactly matched the original building left over from a completed project in the nearby village.

During this building work a sunken well was unearthed which had been filled in by the previous owners. To make an interesting feature close to the house, this was dug out to a shallow depth, a dwarf wall constructed around and a decorative iron top commissioned in case of accidents to visitors. A magnificent stand of *Dierama pulcherrimum*, believed to be the superior form 'Paul Chorium', grows close by. Dierama, appropriately named angel's fishing rod from the graceful way they dip their long stems, are usually planted close to water in order to mirror the drooping effect, but in fact seem to prefer a well drained yet moist soil in either sun or light shade.

The garden plan at Field House is fairly complicated and was never designed on paper, with the owners working from the house and following the classic and well tried pattern of more formality close to the main building, with the wilder areas and the vegetable garden situated further away from habitation.

The owners once propagated plants to sell and the garden still boasts a fifty-foot greenhouse bought second hand and laboriously re-erected. A smaller greenhouse, packed with tender plants, is almost hidden behind two long herbaceous borders which lead to a wooden summer house, and where we had to disturb a group of sleeping ducks to look inside. Again, these beds are packed with plants — *Campanula lactiflora* in purple and white, thalictrums, sidalcea, hardy geraniums, inula, the latter grown to huge proportions as it revelled in the fertile soil and recent damp season. Not to mention large climbing roses such as the rampant 'Bobby James' over every arch and tree. An exciting new plant here is *Lychnis* 'Jenny', a rich pink, and very double — with lots of petals radiating out from a central point.

I have to say that I felt an empathy with the whole picture created. It is a charming mixture of the formal and informal and very much my kind of garden.

Gate Cottage • Cockshutt

A two acre plantsman's garden, full of unusual flowers, trees and shrubs some of special interest to flower arrangers. Open under the National Gardens Scheme, see Yellow Book

Some gardens make an immediate visual impact, others reveal themselves slowly, you could say that this garden does both. Gate Cottage is close to the road with the main garden to the side and rear of the building, the owners finding a small plot mostly consisting of vegetables, unexciting perennials and a derelict orchard when they arrived eighteen years ago. Their policy was to be ruthless, swiftly disposing of all the second rate. Only one huge willow remains close to the house, spared because it was the sole mature tree and whose branches play host to a fifty-foot high rambler rose — 'Paul's Himalayan Musk'. Poorly fruiting but healthy apple trees were also retained in the old orchard, again making excellent props for roses, clematis, honeysuckle and a magnificent golden hop.

The owners first worked outwards from the house, creating a pond, together with terraced screes and raised beds of local Grinshill sandstone. As the soil is heavy clay, these are ideal for plants which enjoy good drainage and are full of interesting treasures. (New to me, is a delightful form of the common heuchera, with very unusual, pale creamy-apricot leaves, *H.* 'Amber Waves'). A further two acres was then purchased to house the rapidly expanding collection of plants, some brought from their small London garden, others bought from good nurseries, the owners always having an eye for the rare and unusual. Flower arrangers visiting the garden will, I am sure, be in raptures when they spy the extraordinary, dull blue/brown delphiniums which have only recently flowered for the first time, after being laboured over for many years. Also the variegated bergenia, to say nothing of the tall

zantedeschia or arum lilies, a clear, glowing green. The latter were bred by that great plantsman Cedric Morris and are no more tender than the common white form. I was under the impression that *Zantedeschia aethiopica* would only survive our winters in water, but the owners of Gate Cottage assure me that deep planting in a damp border works just as well.

At first, coming from a small compact garden, the owners found it difficult to work with long vistas, but little was written down or measured out with string. The garden is more formal close to the house, becoming wilder as one moves away from habitation, though 'wild' is perhaps not the best word to describe any part of this garden. Furthest away from the house are mown paths through a landscape of shrubs and trees containing large island beds, each with its own microclimate according to aspect and varying degrees of shade.

A border devoted to tall subjects that enjoy full sun is planted up with *Onopordum acanthium* — the immense grey Scotch thistle that seeds too generously, cardoon with its deeply dissected leaves, foxgloves and *Crambe cordifolia* with iris in all shades to the fore. A lower bed, also in full sun, has a dramatically colourful border of *Phlox divaricata* and *P. carolina* 'Bill Baker', which the owners state has never let them down whatever the weather. Alliums grow well in the heavy ground, including my special favourites giganteum and aflatunense, as well as a deeper purple form, *A. aflatunense* 'Purple Sensation'. Angelicas in this part of the garden not only include the common kind, but a purple-leafed variety and also a variegated form.

The garden is expanding and evolving. I noticed a grove of eucalyptus which had become too big being heavily lopped in an experimental way to produce 'lollipops'. Conifers abound, many quite new to me. I was particularly drawn to a pendulous chamaecyparis, which looks on first sight like *Picea brewerana*, or Brewer's weeping spruce, but is apparently quicker and easier to grow.

The soil is neutral over the whole of the garden and will grow most plants well. Few rhododendrons are attempted — they of course prefer acid ground — but the owners have found that specimens grafted onto the common ponticum do best, with yakushimanum hybrids the most difficult, perhaps a tip for other gardeners with the same conditions.

I admired the Solomon's seal, thriving so well everywhere, and the peachy-apricot foxgloves, seeding cleverly into just the right places as only foxgloves seem able. Also a large parrotia, quite the best shrub for autumn colour, and a breathtaking *Magnolia sieboldii*, grown as a huge bush, not the usual standard tree. Another lovely foxglove,

which unfortunately doesn't seed quite so well, is *Digitalis parviflora*, as lovely in bud as in flower, though the latter are a knock-out, making a rich, brown, congested spike that stops visitors in their tracks. The owners also drew my attention to a new astrantia called 'Roma', a strong pink of perfect shape, and very floriferous.

Other delights in this plantsman's paradise are a superb *Wisteria sinensis* grown on a pergola. Sinensis is infinitely superior to the more usually seen *W. floribunda*, and points up the owners' philosophy of growing only the best.

Hostas are a speciality at Gate Cottage, and many are of truly enormous size with not a trace of slug damage. We have had a damp season and heavy clay retains moisture, but one hosta in particular, 'Samuri', in two shades of green, looked almost too big to be true.

This is primarily a garden for plants, their needs, peculiarities and welfare come first. But it is also a garden of ever changing shapes and colours, full of interesting individual touches that come together to make an unforgettable picture.

Greythorpe • Gobowen

A medium sized, cottage style garden, with pond and productive kitchen plot.

Open under the National Gardens Scheme, see Yellow Book

Large imposing gardens rarely inspire me, I prefer the private and personal. Greythorpe at Gobowen is just such a garden. From the front it appears to be an ordinary pleasant house in an ordinary — though leafy — road. There is a surprise awaiting you, however, when you venture around the back: three-quarters of an acre of well stocked herbaceous borders, superbly grown shrubs, and a background of tall trees and hedges which give complete privacy, though the owners tell me that they have sixteen neighbours.

The garden has developed over twenty-six years and has seen many changes as tastes have altered, or children grown up and left home. Among the experiments was a tennis court, a large round pond — now a paved sitting out area — and boldly moving large trees when they failed to thrive in their original positions.

The basic design of the garden comprises three separate areas. The largest section, which includes undulating herbaceous beds around a generous lawn, can be seen from the house. To reach the second garden one proceeds under a magnificent *Clematis montana* draped over a pergola and a yew hedge, to a circular lawn with small ornamental trees and a wildlife pond.

The pond is completely fenced with wooden palings for safety and boasts a water wheel and rustic building made of well-weathered timber. I loved the planting around the pond: yellow mimulus, *Iris kaempferi* in a glorious deep purple and red *Lychnis coronaria*, all toned down by the more muted background of *Rosa rugosa* and the dark green of yew. The water lilies were in full flower when we visited, and the owners

have wisely restricted the colour scheme to white — though they do admit a penchant for hot, bright tones throughout the garden. One of their favourite arrangements is a bright red late clematis growing through a fruit tree that produces red apples. The colours are identical, so that it is difficult to tell one from another until actually under the tree.

Although there are some rarities in the garden — I noted an interesting orchid flowered foxglove in white with pink spots — the owners prefer the easy to grow, and commented that although some gardeners ignore the common, plants are usually popular because they are both accommodating and beautiful. Examples of trouble free specimens that I certainly wouldn't be without in my own garden include great clumps of day lilies, *Campanula lactiflora*; large hebes — one so white with flowers it looked like an iced bun — and the invasive, but wonderful, orange alstroemeria. Two forms are grown at Greythorpe, *Alstroemeria* 'Orange King', a rich dark colour, and the paler, well-known variety, seen in cottage gardens everywhere. Both incidentally make excellent cut flowers.

Everything in the garden flourishes with such abundance, I was amazed to learn that the owners use no fertiliser, only home made compost. But they do keep chickens which wander happily around under the plants, no doubt manuring as they go. So much is grown, space is at a premium, even the tall hedges and trees in the garden playing host to climbing plants. Of particular note is a golden hop, which dies down in the winter and can be cut right back to the ground. The owners of Greythorpe manage the tall

hedges by trimming only once a year in the winter, when they are easy to get at without ruining the borders and they are sure no birds are nesting.

The final area of the garden, furthest away from the house, is screened by a hedge of rugosa roses and a huge *Solanum crispum*, the potato vine, in pale mauve. This is the kitchen garden, with currant bushes, gooseberries and raspberries, as well as vegetables.

The whole plot works so well, I was surprised to learn that the garden was designed purely in the owners' heads. They feel it leaves room for impulsive ideas which often arrive only at the 'hands on' stage. It is hard to imagine a more agreeable place to spend a sunny afternoon.

Harnage Farm • Cound

A well stocked farmhouse garden, with glorious views and a conservation wood and wildlife pool
ten minutes walk from the house. Open under the National Gardens Scheme, see Yellow Book

It is difficult sometimes to pin down just what it is that draws one to a particular garden. Plants, setting, just the general ambience of the place. But at Harnage Farm it is easy — I felt in tune with the whole area at once, because it was the kind of garden that I would have created myself. Not too 'designed', but a plot allowed to go its own way, with self-sown valerian and dog daisies.

There is a glorious view over the Shropshire plain to Clee Hill that is made the most of, and lots of delightfully quirky sculptural pieces — tall chimneys from the house, staddle stones, and a stone lion guarding an entrance. I also admired the well placed water features, both comprising spouting masks pouring into raised pools as well as the mature trees, including a venerable cedar and a graceful *Betula pendula* 'Youngii', the latter planted in the perfect position to be admired in the round. Last but not least, the plants, some rare and all beautiful.

The large black and white house dates from the 1920s but fits into its setting well, as it is slightly raised — one approaches it up a sloping drive — and both outbuildings and vegetation tie it into the landscape. Not for the first time, I was amazed at the number of tender specimens now considered hardy in Shropshire, most enjoying the protection of wall or house, but some, including an enormous *Eucalyptus gunnii*, in the open garden. (Planted in 1980, this eucalyptus survived the severe winter of 1982.) It is worth noting that eucalyptus is propagated from seed, and its hardiness does vary according to the altitude at which it was collected in Australia. *Bupleurum fruticosum* is an evergreen shrub with yellow pincushion flowers that I would have hesitated to recommend for a cold, inland county, but is thriving at Harnage Farm. Other tender beauties are a *Buddleia colvilei* with the largest flowers of any hardy outdoor

buddleia in Great Britain; *Euphorbia mellifera*, a superb shrub with huge green shaded flowers and *Cytisus battandieri* not to mention a mimosa!

The owners have farmed the land around the house for thirty-six years, but only became interested in gardening about twenty years ago. It is now a shared passion, growing with the garden as it extended over the years, from a chicken run and rough lawn with only a large cedar, to a retreat full of charm and beauty. There are further plans, I might add, for a new gazebo to over-look the stupendous view in place of a now redundant greenhouse.

A small, sheltered courtyard close to the house is the main sitting out area. It is covered by a wooden pergola, which gives extra room for climbers such as vines, roses and clematis. Among the latter, I was partic-ularly impressed by a dainty viticella called 'Prince Charles'. It is a unique colour, which I can only describe as a pale, pink-mauve. I loved the paving in this area — slabs, gravel and bricks all intermixed, even a small spot of mosaic made from blue and white china pieces. Really tender plants are grown in pots and spend the summer in this sheltered, sunny place, over wintering in the green-house. I noted lemon verbena, the Australian bottle brush, and *Zantedeschia aethiopica* 'Crowborough', the best white arum lily. Once again, however, a tender abutilon was making tremendous growth and flowering well in the open, although I must admit on a sheltered wall.

So many of my favourite plants are grown cottage style at Harnage Farm that it is hard to know where to begin, I kept meeting old friends around every corner. Ballota, its felted, furry leaves beloved by flower arrangers, looked lovely tumbling over a raised bed. Alliums do particularly well in the dryish, stony loam, while the yellow *Allium moly* was making a fine show in June when we visited. Also present is *A.*

christophii, always a show stopper with its exploding firework of a flower.

White mallow is one of the many plants allowed to seed in the flower beds, and helps to tie in the colours, producing an harmo-nious effect throughout the garden. The air is full of the scent of roses, mostly the old types in soft shades of pink and cream, although this perfume is rivalled by that of the pinks, used to edge the herbaceous borders and which also have the most glorious scent. Alpine pinks can be grown from seed and are easier to keep than the named varieties, many of which have lost their vigour through constant vegetative propagation.

The owners of this lovely garden admit that they rarely get away for a holiday. But then, who would want to? This is a garden that will appeal both to the plant lover and to those who just like to be in a beautiful, tranquil place.

Hodnet Hall · Gardens

Over sixty acres of woods, water gardens, choice shrubs, bulbs and herbaceous perennials.

Open daily from April to September inclusive. Please telephone: 01630 084202 for details

Hodnet is a genuine, all year round garden. Many are described as such, but few measure up to the reality. I have visited its sixty-two acres of lakes, rolling landscapes, magnificent trees and inspired plantings on uncountable occasions in every season and discover something new every time. On the latest visit it was a huge rounded block of stone, not unlike a prehistoric megalith, encircled by its own small garden and lying on a bed of ferns. How have I missed it before? It is extraordinarily beautiful and mysterious at the same time. I am informed that it is a glacial boulder of granite which was discovered in one of the smaller ponds in 1960. Hodnet has also managed to keep its personal, 'country house' atmosphere, probably because it has remained in private hands. It was created and developed by the late Brigadier A.G.W. Heber-Percy in the 1920s, and still continues as a family residence.

One of its chief delights is the unstudied blending of the exotic with the ordinary. Rare *Rhododendron augustinii*, perhaps the truest 'blue' rhododendron obtainable, close to wild English bluebells, for example. Then the drifts of daffodils growing simply in grass, but near to an incomparable avenue of magnolias. This too sports *M. soulangiana*, seen in every other suburban garden, but at Hodnet they are the size of forest trees, and interspersed with unusual dark forms such as 'Betty' and the large flowered 'Lennei'. Also 'Pickards Coral', with huge, pink, goblet-shaped blooms and *M. stellata* covered in pure white stars. In May they are followed by the less well known *M. wilsonii*, a gorgeous white with crimson stamens and pendulous, saucer like flowers. Trees range

from ancient oaks, many at the final 'stags horn' phase of their long lives – reminding me irresistibly of 'Ents' — to large exotics such as *Catalpa bignonioides*.

The lakes form the backbone of the garden, however, their banks planted with a representative selection of damp loving marginals, from the gigantic *Gunnera manicata*, with the largest leaves of any hardy plant in the British Isles, to massed ranks of candelabra primulas. The latter are usually in shades of red pink and white, while *P. bulleyana* is a vivid orange. Astilbes, which need slightly less moisture, are planted in blocks of a single colour on the banks of the meandering streams, while the *Iris kaempferi* actually like their feet in the water. I loved the way native plants such as ferns, mimulus and kingcups — the latter in white as well as the common yellow — mingle with the more formal areas of planting. Particularly eye catching in early spring is a group of the variegated flag iris, *Iris laevigata* 'Variegata', as lovely in leaf as flower.

The kitchen garden is separate from the main garden, and, on the way there, one can view the great Tithe Barn dating from the seventeenth century. The isolated building spotted from various view points and situated in the middle of a pasture field is the Dovecote, which was built in 1656. The main house, completed in 1870, has been much altered and is in Elizabethan style. There is also a half-timbered tea room built on the site of the original sixteenth-century hall, containing a unique collection of big game trophies.

A long flight of steps leads from the pools to the Broad Walk and the house, which is situated at the top of a steep slope. There are

superb views from the terrace, and the sloping ground — fertile clay over red sandstone — is mostly planted with Japanese maples, rhododendrons, berberis and kalmias. From the lower rose garden great banks of camellias vie with the magnolias for attention. These are followed by some of the smaller varieties of rhododendron such as *R. orbiculare*, *R. russatum*, and *R. scintillans*. The only one that I am familiar with is scintillans, which has lavender flowers in May and is considered by many gardeners to be one of the best. In August it is the turn of the striking, white flowered *Eucryphia nymansensis*. The latter is not usually considered hardy in Shropshire, but the micro-climate provided by the large sheets of water (which rarely freeze) and the shelter of the trees and the slope, make many exotics possible.

Perhaps when the rhododendrons and azaleas are in full flower is the most spectacular time to visit Hodnet Hall, but in a garden so full of trees, autumn is also not to be missed. The acers are particularly outstanding, not to mention the hydrangeas which provide colour and interest in the difficult month of August.

Memories of Hodnet always remain in the mind long after one has left. After our early spring visit, three in particular are truly unforgettable. The willow-leafed pear, *Pyrus salicifolia*, still very desirable with its narrow silver leaves and elegant habit of growth, covered from head to foot in greeny-white blossom. Then there are the trilliums. I struggle to grow small groups in my own garden; at Hodnet great clumps under leafless trees are perfectly placed, receiving the

essential shade from summer heat by the unfolding canopy overhead. Lastly, an urn, which looks not unlike the top of a Roman column, set in a circle quartered by paths and planted up with hosta.

Hodnet is a garden to delight at any time of the year you care to visit. A place where rare plants, old and well-known varieties, as well as wild flowers are treasured side by side.

Holly Grove • Church Pulverbatch

A one acre formal garden with extensive wildlife area.

Open under the National Gardens Scheme, see Yellow Book

Holly Grove is a garden of about an acre in formal style surrounding a symmetrical late Georgian house of classic shape. What makes it so special, however, is the way a further twenty-five acres of glorious Shropshire countryside has been integrated into the whole, so that it is hard to tell where the garden proper ends and the woods, hedges and meadows begin. Match this with views to the Wrekin, an outstanding collection of unusual plants, one of the best wildlife ponds I have ever seen, alive with dragonflies and birds, not to mention a herd of the old rare breed White Park cattle and the goat-like Soay sheep, and you will understand why this was a favourite among the many splendid gardens we visited.

The owners of Holly Grove have lived there for twelve years and found little of interest in the garden when they moved in, almost the entire scheme having been created literally from a greenfield site. The basic plan is formal, with parallel pleached lime alleys each side of a rose and clematis tunnel, as well as a box parterre facing the front of the house echoing the severe Georgian façade. The divisions between the garden and the surrounding countryside are open, iron, park paling, whilst inside the garden yew hedges and walls divide the area into several enclosed spaces, `a la Hidcote. An old trick, but one that has never been bettered in my opinion when designing a large plot.

When we visited in early August, the roses were over, but the many clematis were proving their worth as the ideal follow-on plant after the ramblers and climbers have had their day. Particularly striking is a superb *Clematis integrifolia*, with smaller flowers than the normal, but extremely floriferous; also the always reliable 'Royal Velours', in velvety, crimson-purple, not to mention the tiny, but exquisite, 'Minuet'. I also admired the underplanting along the pleached lime alley of purple sage mixed with *Allium scorodoprasum* also in purple, and a lovely contrast to the fresh green of the limes.

Hidden at the side of the house is a herb garden quartered by stone paths, sporting box hedging used as a border and with a central bay tree in a pot. Pots are also much in evidence in the pond garden which is sheltered by tall yew hedges — only planted nine years ago, but already well over eight feet tall. The long pond is edged with stones rescued from a demolished wall, while a blue-grey painted seat invites one to sit and watch the fish breaking the surface of the water. As well as the many pots, carefully placed sculpture is used throughout the garden. Naturally weathered and water-worn wooden pieces are at home in the wilder parts, while stone cherubs and urns fit into the more formal areas nearer the house.

Holly Grove boasts two arboretums, one planted some time ago and containing very interesting specimen trees and shrubs such as the rarely seen *Aesculus parviflora*. This small tree has intriguing candlestick flowers — white with red anthers — and is a member of the horse chestnut family which also produces good autumn colour. Alongside I noted the twisted hazel, *Corylus avellana* 'Contorta', and an Australian bottle brush doing extraordinarily well out in the open. Lately, a new arboretum has been started; it is still immature, but, learning by experience, the trees are much further apart and there are plans for another water feature in future years.

Both arboretums are devoted to the more exotic trees and shrubs such as ginkgo, liriodendrons and eucalyptus; the hedgerows around, carefully preserved throughout the entire twenty-five acres, are home to native species. Many of these hedgerows are very ancient and valuable wildlife corridors, as well as containing food trees such as crab apples and guelder rose.

Visitors reach the pond across a wild flower meadow, while casting anxious eyes in the direction of the wide horned cattle peacefully grazing. It is really almost a lake, surrounded by tall alder bushes and overflowing into streams running in a deep ditch. It was alive with blue damselflies when we visited, as well as the larger dragonflies, while woodpeckers flew by overhead and pigeons cooed between sips of water. In the spring the whole area is a carpet of bluebells.

A green lane leads one back to the house, past anxious mother chickens followed by tiny yellow chicks, and an enormous pot-bellied pig enjoying life in a muddy paddock.

Back in the garden are many sitting out places both shady and sunny, including a newly built, hexagonal brick gazebo close to a grove of fruit trees loaded with apples, pears and plums, almost every one playing host to a clematis or rambler rose.

It is hard to imagine a single improvement that could be made to this beautiful garden, which must be every country lover's ideal living space.

Jessamine Cottage • Kenley

A newly developed garden covering about three acres, with large wildlife pond, wild flower
meadow and mixed beds. Open under the National Gardens Scheme, see Yellow Book

Jessamine Cottage is reached in the spring-time by traversing lace-edged lanes over-shadowed by towering hawthorn hedges bowed down by the weight of white blossom. It is a new garden, only begun in 2000, but on a promising site sloping gently away from the house, with the advantage of a ready made natural pond and superb views to Wenlock Edge. The owners are woodland lovers, and have already planted many trees in what will soon be a considerable arboretum.

They returned to this country from New Zealand five years ago, determined to find the right location for their retirement, and, after just one visit to Jessamine Cottage, knew that they had found their ideal house and garden. The feeling was reinforced by a remarkably large New Zealand cabbage palm with a tall trunk and symmetrical rings of branches which already existed close to the back door. I cannot help agreeing with the owners that it must have been 'meant'. Its companion is now a *Sophora tetraptera*, or New Zealand kowhai, brought from that country as a tiny seedling, first planted in a pot, but now braving the winters here with just a plastic bubble wrapping stuffed with straw if really severe weather is forecast. This is a superb tree if you have the right sunny, sheltered spot, with pinnate leaves and large, hanging, tubular yellow flowers. Mine, which came as a gift of seed from a friend in New Zealand, is still in a large pot, but after seeing the lovely specimen at Jessamine Cottage, I am also going to try it out-of-doors.

Most of the land at Jessamine Cottage had been a caravan park, and no time was lost when the owners moved in marking out a lime avenue with a mown path through the

rough grass. As a contrast to the formality of the trees, bulbs were planted in the grass and seeds scattered to encourage a wild flower meadow. There are now dog daisies, butter-cups, ragged robin and campions; but the daffodils — mostly *Narcissus pseudonarcissus*, an old garden variety — have not been a success, gradually disappearing, and other forms will be experimented with in the future.

There was no master plan for the whole garden, the owners designing as they worked, but aware all the time of wanting to include the beautiful landscape around; also having a liking for dappled shade and soft, flowing lines. Two very large island beds make up the bulk of the formal garden alongside the lime avenue, one consisting mostly of herbaceous perennials, but with a few shrubs for structure; the other being largely shrubs, with just a few perennials to fill gaps until the shrubs mature. The shrub

border is looking good, with acers, viburnums and philadelphus thriving in the fertile clay soil, while a huge clump of verbascums steal the show at one end. In the herbaceous bed, the owners have wisely resisted the temptation to plant too close in order to make it look full, utilising a lovely dark blue aquilegia which self-seeds to fill any gaps.

Where a temporary building once stood to administer the caravan park, there is now a wooden tea room or summer house backed by more huge hawthorn hedges. These are covered not only in white blossom, but subtle shades of pale pink. Visitors can then walk across the newly planted arboretum which is filled with some beautiful specimen trees such as *Cornus controversa* 'Variegata', as well as red oaks, acers and native trees. Willows are used where the ground is damp, while the dominant hedge plant is the guelder rose, or *Viburnum opulus*, its flowers a ring of white around a green centre. Alders and lime, already mature when the owners took over, make a shady garden with a small stream, whilst English bluebells, rhododendrons, hydrangea and hosta have already begun to cover the bare ground.

The large pond is in full sun, and must have had a great deal to do with the owners' decision to purchase the property. It is eight feet deep in the centre, with moorhens breeding under the wooden bridge amongst the iris. The latter are mostly *Iris sibirica* and *Iris laevigata* in blue and yellow, while huge clumps of rushes around the edges are reflected in the water.

Near to the house it was decided to introduce a strictly formal note, with beds of lavender 'Hidcote' surrounded by box borders. There are also plans to plant a hedge of espalier pears to divide this area from the rest of the garden. In the vegetable section, three plots for a classic rotation have been constructed, but one consists entirely of fruit which has to be well protected from the abundant bird life. The squirrels also get all the walnuts from the mature tree in a corner, but it is just too big to cover. Shropshire damsons alternate with the hawthorns in the hedges, while wigwams of sweet peas are grown especially for picking. I think the owners have created a perfect setting for their house, as well as blending seamlessly into the surrounding glorious countryside.

Jinlye • Church Stretton

A garden full to overflowing with interesting plants, created out of a bare hilltop twenty-eight years ago
and belonging to a small hotel which welcomes visitors. Please telephone: 01694 723243 for details

To reach Jinlye one goes up a steep lane — and up, and up, for Jinlye is situated high in the Shropshire hill country. This is a mountainous landscape in miniature, with glorious views in all directions, sometimes purple, sometimes green, sometimes blue and with the rocky outcrops of the Stiperstones apparently at the same level as the house. The great disadvantage of this setting is of course the fierce winds, and the owner has inevitably had to sacrifice the view in some directions to wind breaks of conifers.

The house fits snugly into the landscape as it is an old farm, now much extended, but in a sympathetic style. Sheep graze right up to the boundary fence, while banks of wild heather make the hills around appear part of the garden. The actual layout is on a slight slope, but because it is situated right on the top of a gently rounded summit, it is nowhere steep and lends itself to herbaceous beds, fine, well-shaped shrubs, trees and even a laburnum tunnel.

The owner has gardened on the site since 1976. I was shown pictures of the original farm and the change is nothing short of extraordinary, as in the pictures it is surrounded by bare, bleak hillside, with not a tree or a flower in sight.

After the alterations to the house were completed, thoughts could turn to the design of the garden. The workmen left great piles of rubble, as well as much usable building stone from demolished outbuildings, so a simple solution was to surround the rubble with dwarf walls, spreading it out to provide good drainage and topping off with horse manure and soil. These circular raised beds are now utilised to grow alpines, and other low, spreading plants to great effect, fitting in well with the hilly terrain.

One very large raised bed, right in front of the house, was planted up with slow growing dwarf conifers which have now reached some size. They would be easy to deal with were they not draped with long swags of the bright red *Tropaeolum speciosum*. This superb climber, so difficult to grow south of Scotland — it likes cool, damp conditions and acid soil — has looped itself all around the dark green conifers, the

perfect background to show off the violent scarlet of its flowers.

The garden boasts many sitting out places, and as Jinlye is run as a small hotel, visitors enjoy the garden quite as much as the owner. Many of the raised beds are especially appreciated by disabled guests, who, from a wheelchair, can get a close look at all the plants.

The scree garden at the rear of the house looked particularly beautiful when we saw it in early July, the dwarf campanulas overflowing onto paths and over stones. All the miniatures are choice — I have never found any campanula I didn't admire and covert for my own garden — and at Jinlye there are violets, blues and whites, smothered in tiny blooms. One of the best is *Campanula poscharskyana* which is never without a flower from May through to autumn. *C. garganica*, is also very easy to grow in any position where it gets sun, and *C. carpatica*, which makes more of a clump, can be very easily raised from seed. A real tiny which does well in the sharp drainage is *C. pulla*, which comes in both single or double forms.

Another rare tropaeolum in a sheltered raised bed, the frustratingly difficult *T. polyphyllum*. This nasturtium has small, orange-yellow flowers set off by minute, blue-grey leaves. I have never managed to get it going in my own garden, but at Jinlye it is romping away. I can only liken all the creeping, interlaced dwarf plants in the scree and raised beds to a form of embroidery on canvas, but using flowers and leaves instead of silks.

In the herbaceous borders, meconopsis grow very well as one would expect — they like the same conditions as tropaeolum — but I also noted all the tall campanulas, ligularia, *Geranium striatum* — a particular favourite of mine with mauve and white striped flowers — the gorgeous double blue *Geranium himalayense* 'Plenum', aquilegias, pink delphiniums, and a superb mauve

penstemon, much like a darker form of 'Stapleford Gem'.

All the trees in the garden looked wonderful considering the bleak conditions, well rounded with no wind damage. I particularly admired a variegated Tulip tree, brought back from the dead in 2002 the owner told me, and now flourishing, as well as a heavily pruned paulownia, its enormous leaves and foxglove-shaped flowers immaculate. Not a tree I would have recommended for a windy site, but thriving at Jinlye.

The owner now gardens alone and considered moving last year, but is still there. It must be very difficult to leave what I can only describe as a life-long labour of love.

Laburnum Road • Telford

A suburban garden with every imaginable feature one can think of packed into a tiny area.

Because of parking problems and the garden's diminutive size, this is not open to the public

The smaller the garden, the better the design and the more meticulous the maintenance has to be. The owner of the outstanding garden at Laburnum Road never draws anything on paper, but often sits and thinks for months before proceeding with any alterations or new planting scheme. Then it has to be submitted to the other half of the partnership for her approval. The process seems to work, as the whole garden is an object lesson in how to get the most out of a tiny space.

There is very little lawn, most of the plot at the back of the house consisting of narrow, intricate paths drawing you on to explore further, and providing a surprise around every corner in the shape of shrubs and unusual trees; coupled with numerous tiny streams leading to a central pond. There is even a stone bridge, a summer house and a vegetable and fruit corner.

Although the garden is situated close to a busy main road, and with many near neighbours, complete privacy is guaranteed by high hedges and 'fedges' — that useful combination of fence covered with climbers such as ivy, which provides the best tall, narrow, division where space is limited.

Most of the lower planting is herbaceous perennials, with careful use of smaller shrubs, all selected to fit the confines of the plot. A few annuals are used however, to fill in gaps, as well as in pots around the house. Especially noteworthy here are the fuchsia and a superb datura, or angel's trumpet, quite six or seven feet high. The latter is an excellent conservatory subject, though it can be placed outside in high summer. It has large, hanging, white flowers, which are highly scented. They turn up at the corners, giving the whole plant an oriental air.

Another clever idea in the limited space is the use of bamboo. Some clumps are very tall, but do not overshadow other plants nearby as they are light and open, as well as being easily controlled.

The owners created the garden from scratch over forty-four years ago, the house

being brand new when they moved in just after they were married. Early on very little money was spent, most stock being grown from seed, or picked up for a song from Woolworths. A huge *Magnolia x soulangiana*, its flowers white, streaked with mauvey/pink, was enjoying a second flowering when we visited in August and it was hard to believe that this handsome tree was a 'Woolworth's special'.

Although the middle of the garden is open in aspect, most of the surrounds are quite shady. Here many interesting hostas flourish, as do epimediums and heuchera. Both the former are cut back when they are past their best to allow the heuchera more room, getting good value again from the limited space.

The garden is full of sitting out places, my favourite being a covered wooden seat almost hidden by clematis and overlooking the pond. There are many arches and trel-

lises, which are also ideal for the smaller clematis, such as 'Etoile Rose', delightful in colour — a deep pink — and shape, with tiny, turned back petals.

I noted a good specimen of the golden elm, *Ulmus* 'Wredei', but was more intrigued by *U. procera* 'Argenteovariegata', which has leaves splashed with silvery white and, like 'Wredei', appears to be resistant to Dutch elm disease.

I can only describe the vegetable corner as amazing, to say nothing of the many varieties of apples, pears and plums all grown on single stems, or trained as espaliers against the fence to maximise production. The soil underneath is planted with salad crops such as lettuce in place of flowers.

It was fascinating to learn that this garden won the Shropshire Garden of the Year Competition several years ago. The owners then completely redesigned it — and won again. Need I say more?

Limeburners · Ironbridge

A large shrub and tree garden planned to attract wildlife.

Open under the National Gardens Scheme, see Yellow Book

Limeburners is situated high on a steep wooded slope overlooking the Ironbridge Gorge with views across the Severn to the opposite bank, the only disadvantage of this spectacular site coming from the extreme poverty of the swiftly draining soil. It was once a rubbish tip for black foundry waste, dumped on a bed of limestone similar in geological makeup to the nearby Wenlock Edge. Wisely — as herbaceous perennials dislike both the lack of nutrients and the tendency to drought — the owners have opted for a magnificent range of shrubs and trees, which not only suit the conditions but also provide sustenance for butterflies, dragonflies, birds and insects; to say nothing of the Pipistrelle bats which live in the attics of the house and make it dangerous to open bedroom windows at night! During our visit, harsh croaks from overhead that sounded like flying frogs proved to be members of the local raven population which also visit the garden, while large mammals such as badgers and foxes lurk in the surrounding undergrowth.

Badgers are in fact not entirely welcome, chiefly because they create havoc on the large lawn which forms the main axis of the garden, sloping gently, then steeply, to a wild meadow and long oval pond. An ingenious device consisting of a low (about one foot high) electric fence around the entire lawn has succeeded in keeping them at bay, but evidence of their digging in the wild meadow and the grass paths through the trees and shrubs, points to a sizeable badger population.

Also manifest — and much more welcome — are dozens of butterflies which are attracted to the numerous buddleias in the garden. (A useful tip is to prune the buddleias heavily in late April so that they are in full flower later in the year when the butterflies are on the wing and require nectar.) Among the buddleias I noted several rarer specimens — although the butterflies of course couldn't care less which kind they are — including *Buddleia* 'Dartmoor', with extra long, heavy mauve racemes, as well as all the usual white, pink and dark purple davidii forms, the latter of course, being the one most gardeners are familiar with. *B. x weyerana* is a strange hybrid between *B. globosa* and a davidii, with ball-shaped flowers in an unusual mauve-orange shade. I am not an expert on the butterfly family, but was thrilled to spot a Silver Washed Fritillary and have a Purple Hairstreak pointed out to me close to the buddleia grove, though it apparently breeds on the surrounding oak trees. In the wild meadow — which is cut twice a year and has mown paths — Speckled Wood butterflies and the more common Meadow Brown were moving between the late thistles, the tall, pale blue chicory and the white scabious.

The whole garden covers about thirteen acres, but only two are intensively cultivated, the remainder being made up of natural woodland, scrub and steep limestone banks. I remember the owners telling me that they planted out most of the trees and shrubs in the notorious drought year of 1976, but, in spite of this early set back, the garden is now fully mature with a representative selection of shrubs and trees well suited to the conditions. A grouping which caught my eye immediately was *Berberis* 'Rose Glow' underneath a golden *Robinia pseudoacacia* 'Frisia'. Also a large *Colutea arborescens* or bladder senna in pale yellow. I used to grow the apricot form *C. orientalis*, and both are fine, trouble-free shrubs easily propagated from seed. Nicandra, or the shoe fly plant, is an annual which swiftly makes a large bush and is beloved by insects. It has delightful little mauve flowers, and again is easily raised from seed. An extraordinary tree in the garden, is *Aralia elata*, with huge pinnate leaves and panicles of large branching white flowers late in the year.

In such shallow, poor soil I was surprised to see so many hydrangeas doing well (they usually prefer a damper medium) but care has been taken to provide the shade they require, and superb specimens of *H. aspera villosa* with lilac-blue flowers and hairy leaves, as well as the pure white *H. paniculata*, were alive with insects. Of special note is a waist high specimen called 'Red Start', a truly fabulous, very dark pink with a lighter centre, and which has been added to my list of 'must have' plants.

The garden is much shadier than I remembered from years before, now that the many trees are approaching maturity, and several have to be removed on a regular basis to open up new areas of the garden to light. A huge Atlas cedar makes a spectacular single specimen on the big lawn however, as does a *Betula jacquemontii*. Close to the house a grove of rare birch, *B. nigra*, *B. utilis* and *B. alba septentrionalis*, together with acers and *Prunus serrula* have replaced some fruit trees, while *Acer griseum* in solitary state marks the other side of the house.

There is a small formal pond close to the main building, though the garden boasts a superb wildlife pond tightly planted right up to its edges with shrubs and perennials. These afford cover for frogs and other amphibians, as well as making the water look part of the landscape. Also in this area are large groupings of *Acanthus spinosus*, with uncountable flower heads, Japanese anemones and clumps of the dark red day lily 'Stafford', all of which gradually give way to the wild meadow below which, late in the year, is full of ornamental seed heads.

Gardens can look very tired in August, but the clever choice of shrubs which suit the conditions mean that Limeburners always has something of interest to enchant visitors both human and wild.

Little Heldre • Buttington

Nearly two acres of steeply sloping hillside garden, comprising a terraced area, wild dingle with stream and glorious views. Open under the National Gardens Scheme, see Yellow Book

I have visited and described many gardens in hilly terrain all over Shropshire and the Border Counties, but never one on quite so steep a slope as Little Heldre. The owners informed me that in its one-and-three-quarter acres, the lowest point is at six hundred feet, whilst the upper boundary is at eight hundred. The only patches of level ground in the whole garden are those on which the house rests, and a good sized lawn on the north side of the building.

When the owners moved in five years ago, they found a neglected garden with few interesting plants except for some over-mature trees and shrubs. There was evidence however of some work in the past and they wisely waited a year to see what would 'come up', discovering a network of old paths choked with weeds and grass as well as many bulbs. Almost everything one sees at Little Heldre now is the work of the present occupants, and one can only admire the way they

have brought the whole difficult terrain under control in such a short time scale.

The house sits in the middle of the plot, and the garden falls naturally into two main areas. The first is a formal terraced portion leading up from the house with grass, many unusual shrubs under-planted with herbaceous perennials, as well as a well placed pond, further herbaceous beds, a summer-house (moved to take advantage of vistas over the Shropshire plain as far as the Berwyn mountains) and a unique pergola sloping steeply over a long flight of steps.

The other part of the garden, known as The Dingle, is reached over the aforementioned lawn, and is divided from the main plot by a low berberis hedge. It is a complete contrast to the upper garden, though again contains precipitous paths and steep slopes. This time, however, visitors are led through a natural landscape of native trees, bluebells and ferns, with a tiny but swiftly moving

stream rushing through from one end to the other. Several bridges have been constructed, and there are further plans for more wild flower planting, roses as ground-cover, and an ambitious idea to dam the stream creating a large pool with possible cascades. This whole area provides a lovely, green, sheltered contrast to the open, sunny, colourful garden above.

The soil in the garden is mainly a neutral light loam which grows rhododendrons and other lime haters well. The owners make their own compost, shredding all they cut down or dig up, and storing it in four huge bins. One unusual characteristic of the site is that some parts are very damp where springs surface, whilst others have a tendency to dry out — an occupational hazard when gardening on a hillside.

The pond, which lies in a hollow near the top of the garden, is natural, but has been recently terraced, the soil held back by fence posts driven into the ground close together. Many different materials are used for terracing throughout the garden, including railway sleepers and stone from a local quarry. The owners dealt with the slope bit by bit, working out from the house and completing one section at a time, planting as they went, and renovating old shrubs by judicious pruning. Although they claim not to be expert plantspeople, just putting in what they like or what suits the ground. The choice throughout the garden showed a true eye for the beautiful and unusual.

Some parts which especially appealed to me were the long herbaceous border at the top of the garden — all herbaceous so as not to hide the view from the summerhouse — with well staked peonies (pea sticks are recommended) dianthus and drifts of dogwood. Other good ideas included *Ribes speciosum* with its hanging red flowers trained on the side of the pergola like an espalier apple, and a dead tree covered in the glorious, rampant, white climbing rose, 'Seagull'.

At the back of the house the hill has been excavated to make a sunny patio, and a round moon gate of old brick allows another glimpse of the stupendous view; silent cars and lorries the size of dinky toys moving along the main road many miles away. I loved the large pittosporum serving as a prop for my favourite blue macropetala clematis, also the great banks of heather and giant clumps of phormium. All the walls and the house are covered in climbing roses and clematis. I especially admired the white montana in this area, with a distinctive scent as well as a beautiful flower.

One could go on — the gunnera with its fascinating flower heads, just the right choice for a difficult, damp ditch, the hebe clipped to resemble a quirky animal, or the lovely grove of birch, rowan and oak, with bulb-filled rough grass beneath in the middle of the formal terracing, creating just the right restful note. All one can say is, come and see it for yourself.

Lower Hall · Worfield

A beautifully designed garden packed with unusual plants, surrounding a sixteenth-century Tudor house on the River Worfe. Open under the National Gardens Scheme, see Yellow Book

The grounds at Lower Hall fall into two distinct areas: a series of formal gardens around the architecturally distinguished house, and a wilder part with sweeping lawns and magnificent mature trees centred on the River Worfe. It must be very unusual to have an important waterway actually cutting one's plot in half, no matter how extensive, but the owners of Lower Hall have made the most of their asset, diverting the main river into a network of smaller channels and ponds, as well as bridging them several times in both wood and stone.

The four-acre garden is dominated, however, by the superb, timber-framed manor house in weathered grey wood and white plaster. It consists of a complicated series of gables and bays with a central turret, and a number of brick and red sandstone chimneys, as well as numerous windows sashed in the eighteenth century. A single storey block juts out from the house providing one side of the enclosed vegetable garden. This is contemporary with the main building, and is thought to have once been a brew house, store rooms, or servants' quarters. Although the house dates from 1550 it had been completely rendered in Georgian times — exposed timbering then being considered inferior. When the present owners moved in over forty years ago they began a programme of work which included a total renovation of both house and garden to their former glory.

Not the least of Lower Hall's charms is that it lies at the centre of a delightful village (though complete privacy is assured by the high sandstone walls all around the plot) and within eye and ear shot of St. Peter's church; one hears not only the music of the river, but the sound of church bells and the cooing of doves from the spire overlooking the house. The garden designer Lanning Roper had a hand in the original plans for Lower Hall, but his ideas were adapted and modified by the owners, who are still very much 'hands on' gardeners, managing the whole area with only one employee. They are constantly planting and improving, using the hose-pipe technique to lay out island beds and picking up new, exciting plants from Chelsea; including (in 2004) the rarely seen dwarf horse chestnut, *Aesculus nana.*

One side of the river is acid the other alkaline, and this has dictated the planting scheme, with magnolias in variety flourishing on the far bank. (Rhododendrons were also once a feature in this area, but abandoned after a disastrous flood followed by freezing in 1982.) Notable specimens include *Magnolia obovata* with huge flowers and leaves, as well as *M. x highdownensis*, very like *M. sieboldii*, but with a purple central cone. Large stands of trillium and gaultheria provide good ground-cover, as do the more common, but none the less beautiful, hardy geraniums. Three *Betula nigra* or river birch are a sight to behold with their wonderful tattered bark, and are recommended for damp ground. In fact, the entire garden is full of outstanding trees: a pink *Catalpa fargesii duclouxii*, a tulip tree (in full flower when we visited) and a superb specimen of *Cornus kousa chinensis* loaded down with white blooms in solitary splendour on the main lawn. Many of the taller trees are used as props for vigorous climbing roses such as *Rosa brunonii*, the Himalayan musk rose, a rampant climbing species with scented white flowers in June.

The river of course is central to this part of the garden, and all the best damp loving marginals flourish in the fertile moist soil. Good foliage is valued at Lower Hall, and I noted filipendula, arum lilies in white, astilbe, *Iris sibirica*, hostas and ligularia, as well as a whole small island devoted to candelabra primulas. I loved the way one could get really close to the river by negotiating the stone steps close to ancient iron machinery from a long demolished mill. Here the water rushes over a weir shaded by trees and under a wooden bridge before emptying into a large pool, then narrowing again to take a further step down on its journey out of the garden.

Close to the house the atmosphere is completely different, dictated by the hall and outbuildings as well as the high walls of stone and weathered brick. Here the design is formal, with profuse planting in mixed borders of shrubs, roses and hardy perennials. Paths are also of brick, the dark green of well clipped yew alternating with the dull red background of sandstone and brick. The tree peonies and ceanothus were spent when we visited, but *Abutilon vitifolium* in mauve and white, as well as rugosa roses and vast

bushes of pink cistus were taking their place. Again I was impressed by the attention to detail and the emphasis on interesting foliage, from the purple sage overflowing the paths, to the stand of giant Scotch thistle topping a ten foot high wall.

Mention must also be made of the many well-placed sculptures and ornaments found throughout the garden, and reflecting modern taste in the shape of a round millstone-like granite piece by Tony Twentyman, as well as the delightful cherubs, fountains, urns and stone seats that fit so well close to the Tudor house.

Gates in rose-hung walls lead to further hidden gardens, while a walk under a metal pergola takes visitors to a shaded sitting out place. Nearby, an old orchard contains not only fruit trees but more roses, as well as scented shrubs such as orange-blossom and lilac. A tiny fountain garden enclosed by tall yew hedges looped with tropaeolum in vermillion, is set off by the imposing house wall. Hot and still in the summer, it also shelters camellias for winter colour, and a tier of stone steps flanked by containers.

It is hard to imagine how this wonderful site could be laid out in a better way; house, setting and plants create a perfect picture. The English country garden *par excellence*, a garden one can walk around, take tea in, or just sit and admire.

Millichope Park · Munslow

Classic English parkland around a fine house, with outstanding trees, wide lakes and beautiful vistas.

Open under the National Gardens Scheme, see Yellow Book

The avenue which leads to Millichope Park has to be one of the most dramatic and romantic approaches to a grand house in Shropshire, with deeply cut sandstone cliffs towering above the path, all overhung with strands of ivy. Visitors burst out of the gloom into a classic landscape of lakes, tall trees and sloping lawns, with the great house dominating the scene at the top of the hill overlooking the water and parkland. One of the best places to see mature specimens of all our native and introduced trees are the parks and gardens surrounding important houses, and Millichope has more than its fair share. To name just a few of the biggest and most imposing, the park contains some of the largest yews, cypress, firs, cedars, Scots pine, copper beech, holm oak, London planes and oriental planes in the country. These are distributed around a parkland covering thirteen acres in the beautiful Corvedale valley with views as far as Brown Clee. Most of the trees were planted in the late nineteenth century, are now fully mature, and are at their most impressive height and spread.

Millichope was designed by Edward Haycock of Shrewsbury in the eighteen-forties, very much in the grand manner, with an imposing façade of Ionic columns constructed out of severe grey stone. The effect is lightened, however, by a magnificent show of annuals in a variety of urns and baths decorating the balustraded terrace. These include fuchsia, diascia, petunias and lobelia, all complementing the containers of weathered stone, marble, rusted iron and terracotta. Beneath the tall fluted columns the wall which supports them is hidden behind a line of *Magnolia grandiflora* trained against the stone, benefiting both from the south-westerly aspect and the protection of the house. When we visited in late July, one enormous, scented cream flower, still hung among the polished, dark green leaves.

The view from the terrace is a picture book landscape of water, trees and distant hills; but the eye is immediately drawn to a temple, or Rotunda, with Ionic columns, set on a sandstone bluff across the lake. It predates the house, and is perfectly placed to reflect in the still, calm water below. The entrance is reached by climbing a steep little hill along a path of mown grass with rough grass further afield full of wild flowers, and, in the spring time, drifts of early bulbs. There are banks crowded with *Hypericum* 'Hidcote' in glossy yellow, set off by every shade of green that one can imagine from the trees around. The temple itself however, is backed by a single, enormous, cedar of Lebanon; its dark green, almost black horizontal branches and leaves, a wonderful foil for the upright, grey columns of the temple.

Although this is a man-made landscape, nature has had her way in the lower lake, filling it with bulrushes and reeds. The larger lake though, has been left to the swans, reflections and a huge patch of pink water lilies. These are as large as lotus blossoms

with rings of yellow stamens, all set in a carpet of round green leaves floating on the water. There is an island of foliage plants in the main lake: rheums, red acers and hosta predominating, echoed by a great stand of gunnera on the bank. Dragonflies of all kinds swoop among the flag iris and meadow sweet, while ducks and moorhens lead battalions of young across from one side to the other, the sound of running water as one stretch empties into another always present in the distance wherever one walks within sight of the lakes.

The park is also full of a great variety of superb garden ornaments, including two bulbous, dark granite elephants, who decorate the steps leading to a side door. Near the house, a stone shepherd and shepherdess are placed in a setting of lawn and trees, adding a focal point to an otherwise uninteresting corner.

Millichope is chiefly a garden of green vistas and trees, but I very much enjoyed the square, interlocking gardens hidden by high hedges, close to the house. The first one is very simple, consisting of two oblong, parallel pools filled with water lilies. This leads into another plot with a central lawn, each corner bed full of herbaceous perennials and shrubs, such as roses, alstroemeria, phlox, astilbe, white epilobium and hardy geraniums. A border closer still to the rear of the house contains a line of white roses, while walls play host to *Eccremocarpus scaber* in red; the deciduous, summer flowering *Ceanothus* 'Gloire de Versailles', phlomis and *Clematis rehderiana*. These are set off by bushes of white potentilla, berberis, philadelphus and Penstemon 'Sour Grapes'.

Millichope is a garden filled with the atmosphere of the past, and although it is difficult to relate its wide acres to today's smaller, more compact gardens, still has much to offer with its visually breathtaking landscape.

Moortown • near Wellington

A sophisticated cottage garden owned by a dedicated plantsman, packed with unusual treasures.

Open under the National Gardens Scheme, see Yellow Book

Shropshire is full of superb gardens big and small which fill one with admiration and awe, but which one would not necessarily want to own. Moortown is extensive, packed with rare plants and also fills me with admiration, but has the added advantage of being just the kind of garden that I could live with. There is something about the ambience of the place which soothes the spirit, whilst the profusion of unusual plants, from the gigantic copper beech at the entrance, to the myriads of uncommon, self-sown aquilegia, must make visiting plantaholics smile from ear to ear.

I have described Moortown as a sophisticated cottage garden, though the house it surrounds is far from a cottage, being a dignified, red brick, late Georgian farmhouse. Most of the outbuildings and walls are contemporary with the main building and constructed either of the same warm brickwork or local pinkish sandstone. Around the house are several distinct areas marked off by walls and shrubs. A sunless paved garden under the copper beech has a staddle stone centre piece, with the shade loving *Geranium phaeum* dominating the planting. Then there is a wide gravelled drive full of self-sown seedlings such as nepeta and poppies, with many mature trees and shrubs including a superb ceanothus on the house wall. Also enjoying the shelter are a choisya, a laburnum with extra long racemes, and a Mount Etna broom. Three more huge staddle stones make dramatic, abstract sculptural shapes, while an old millstone is used as an all-weather table. On the house itself, climbing roses and clematis reach to the eaves. A small lawned plot contains a seat under a magnolia with views over flat fields to the Wrekin, while a herd of cows graze peacefully behind a low wall.

The main garden lies across a lawn and is separated from the house by an evergreen hedge. It is laid out with alternate lines of border and grass paths, the middle portion overhung with a long iron arbour or pergola rescued from a demolished house nearby and covered from end to end with climbers. These are mostly vines, clematis, roses, honeysuckle and the five leaf form of *Akebia quinata*, which has fragrant, reddish-purple flowers in April, and a vigorous, twining habit of growth.

At the end of the garden a large semicircular bed is bisected by narrow paths, and contains an eclectic mixture of the common and the rare. Perhaps the most dramatic sight when we visited was a huge example of *Ferula communis* 'Gigantea'. This plant is about six feet high, with rounded clumps of flowers in a wonderful golden yellow. The foliage is light and airy, like a typical fennel, and at Moortown it is backed by a silver leaf pear, creating an unforgetable picture in silver and gold. Another old cottage garden plant not often met with nowadays is the spreading lily, *Lilium pyrenaicum*, which behaves like no other, running through the soil and creating new bulblets as it goes. It has lovely foliage, yellow or orange shaded 'Turk's cap' flowers and must be one of the easiest of all the lilies to grow, although it does like sharp drainage.

A garden such as Moortown is very labour intensive and can quickly become overgrown, but to me the self-seeding and the profusion of plants, all spilling out of their allotted positions, just adds to its charm. The only touches of formality come from the sandstone walls and steps, as well as the iron fences, seats and arches, which seem to stitch the garden together. I also appreciated the way large architectural plants are used as corner pieces, marking the ends of borders with *Stipa gigantea*, libertia, and in one instance, yet another staddle stone.

Every variety of ornamental elder known is grown in this garden, including the dazzling yellow 'Sutherland Gold'. Other shrubs looking good in late May were the variegated dogwood, *Cornus alba* 'Variegata', and the pimpinellifolia roses. Among the herbaceous perennials, everything suitable for sun or shade was bursting out of the border: tall thalictrums, Soloman's seal in its rare, variegated form, hardy geraniums, oriental poppies, astrantia; all jostling for space with self-sown Welsh poppies, Bowles' golden grass and white stocks. The whole area is surrounded by oaks, beeches, and chestnuts in full flower.

Narrow side paths lead off to quiet green oases, one containing a weathered gazebo, others climbing roses or wrought-iron arches covered in yet more climbers, including many variegated ivies. The garden once boasted a collection of rare tulips, but these were found to be too time consuming, and now most of the comprehensive collection of bulbs can be found in the main garden, with rare snowdrops (a speciality) and tulips of course, predominating.

Another much admired touch is a line of the giant hogweed — only noticed when one is leaving the garden — perfectly placed against a brick stable wall; all green and with a border to themselves. This is yet another example of how to combine a natural feel with the underlying structure in a garden which, for me, never puts a foot wrong.

4 The Mount Cottage · Shrewsbury

A large town garden surrounding a distinguished Georgian house, packed with rare and unusual plants.

Open occasionally for local charities; please telephone: 01743 354540 for details

One comes to a town garden with certain preconceived ideas — that it will be compact, sheltered, perhaps a little claustrophobic with high walls, your ears assaulted by traffic noise. At The Mount Cottage, every one of these expectations is overturned. The garden is large, and, in spite of its close proximity to Shrewsbury town centre, surrounded by other gardens full of mature trees, a long drive bordered by thickly planted shrubs and fruit trees, while the fourth side overlooks a long peaceful reach of the River Severn alongside the West Midland Show Ground.

The house is situated next door to Darwin's birthplace, The Mount, part of the steep bank leading down to the Severn at the back of the house being part of the old Mount Estate. The house was built in 1790 (before Darwin's birthplace existed) and is a typical Georgian house of beautiful mellow brick. When we visited in early May, the entire front of the building, as well as part of the side elevation, was covered by a truly sensational wisteria in full bloom. The contrast between the subtle mauve of the wisteria and the brickwork was little short of perfection, its twisted, ancient grey stems almost as interesting as the glorious flowers.

The owners of The Mount Cottage have gardened on the site for thirty-two years, finding very little to work with when they moved in, apart from the wisteria and a large weeping cherry, the latter also still very much alive and blooming. One of the first problems faced was access. Planning permission was granted for a long drive, which gradually winds uphill to the house and is bordered by a fascinating collection of shrubs and small trees. Drainage is perfect because of the steep slope, with phlomis, tender rosemaries, *Acer palmatum* 'Dissectum' and *Daphne x burkwoodii*, all flourishing. (The owners informed me that because the female half of the partnership is named Daphne, there are over forty planted in the garden.) The original idea was to use the shrubs as ground-cover, but they now provide a compact, close mass of foliage and flowers which must make maintenance easier on such a steep slope. One very tall conifer, right at the top of the drive, is the beautiful and elegant *Picea omorika* 'Pendula', covered in May with pale green new growth.

A formal water garden lies to the side of the house, with raised ponds full of water hyacinth. A natural wildlife feature was contemplated but, because of the close proximity of the house, square ponds built with bricks from a demolished wing were used. The bricks were also utilised to build walls throughout the garden, all blending with the house and dividing the plot into two areas.

The front lawn is surrounded by sheltered beds, which means that many plants not usually considered hardy in Shropshire can be attempted. *Magnolia grandiflora* for example, and the rare and tender *Buddleia agathosma* — pale mauve with a delightful scent. A huge pittosporum grows hard against the tall brick wall, but many others flourish in pots, as well as a lovely *Acer palmatum* 'Beni-Naiki'; recommended by the owners as a good one for a large container. Unusually for a town garden, badgers are a problem with a big set in the bank leading down to the river. A partial solution is feeding them, the idea being that this will at least prevent them digging up the lawn.

Many unusual herbaceous perennials can be found in this part of the garden and in a gravelled area close to the ponds. Hardy geraniums, gentiana, *Anemone pulsatilla* and the dwarf *Iris* 'My Jewel', as well as a superb dark purple iris with a blue flash, unfortunately of unknown variety. Good shrubs include the now rarely seen *Hebe hulkeana*, with lavender-blue racemes much larger than normal, as well as *Eucryphia glutinosa*.

Walking through a wrought-iron gate into the rear garden, one is struck by the wonderful view through the tree canopy of the river winding peacefully in the valley below. Here the walls and shrubs are hung with early flowering clematis such as *Clematis alpina* 'Willy' and *C. montana sericea*, while huge examples of the tree peony, *P. lutea ludowii* and camellias are sheltered by the house. An experimental peat garden, planned in ascending tiers was attempted in the past — throughout the garden the pH is fairly neutral — but badgers and honey fungus have made maintenance difficult. It is now devoted to small trees such as acers and magnolias, under-planted with dwarf yakushimanum rhododendrons.

There are several unusual roses, including a favourite of mine, 'Canary Bird', with single yellow flowers. Perhaps the most extraordinary is a thirty-year-old *Rosa roxburghii normalis* with pale pink flowers, in the centre a mass of golden stamens and, later, large hips covered with prickles. I was interested to see the honeysuckle *Lonicera x americana*, not subject to black-fly, and to hear the recommendation that it is planted away from a wall to keep this pest at bay.

Between the house and the drive is a soft fruit garden with several fruit trees, all except 'James Grieve' planted by the owners. These, together with the winding drive, cushion the house from traffic noise. There is a small greenhouse for cuttings, and treasures in this part of the garden include *Edgeworthia chrysantha* which has fragrant yellow flowers in February, as well as that rarest, most desirable tree peony *P. suffruticosa* 'Rockii'. This wonderful plant, pure white with a black blotch, must be at the top of every keen and knowledgeable gardener's list, and is but one example of the diversity of rare plants to be found in this superb garden.

The Old Farmhouse · Boningale

A child-friendly cottage garden around a timber-framed, seventeenth-century house, with walks over meadows and newly planted woodland. Open under the National Gardens Scheme, see Yellow Book

Looking over the low, pink sandstone wall curving around the front garden at The Old Farmhouse, one is irresistibly reminded of Mirabel Osler's famous garden book, *A Small Plea for Chaos*. Chaos there certainly is a plenty; a glorious uncontrived mixture of colour and scent spilling over cobbled paths, tumbling along walls, and climbing through hedges and trees. The Old Farmhouse itself is an essential element in the picture. A typical Shropshire yeoman-farmer's Tudor house, constructed from every type of building material that one can think of: great blocks of pink sandstone matching the curved wall fronting on to the lane, grey weathered wood with mellow brick nogging infill, the upper stories rendered in cream plaster, and the whole set off by an ancient tiled roof. The garden compliments the house to perfection, in that it must be most people's idea of the ultimate cottage garden.

The tiny front plot between the house and the lane has no lawn, only a flagged and cobbled path dividing the jumble of flowers bursting out of the beds on either side. They are close packed as befits these simple, easy-to-grow plants, and include such favourites as nepeta in mauvey-blue, valerian, thalictrum and campanulas. Roses hang their heads over the wall, while the scent of the old bush *Rosa rugosa* 'Roseraie de l'Hay, is detectable even in the lane outside.

The main garden to the side of the house consists of a large oblong lawn with wide borders. When we visited in late June these were dominated by the daisy *Anthemis tinctoria* in several shades, from pale cream to vibrant yellow. They have self-seeded in all the borders, making for a consistent, but completely unstudied background to the other colours. Self-seeding is encouraged in the best cottage gardens, seedlings seem to thrive when they have chosen their own positions.

This is a family garden for people to enjoy in their own way, and I thought the children's swings with the supporting posts used as props for the golden hop and clematis an

excellent idea. There is a playhouse hidden among foliage in the border, and space for vegetables outlined by low box hedges at the top of the garden. Shrubs are small and neat throughout, hebes, lavender and pruned buddleias predominating; though tall conifers edge the garden where it meets the lane. Some of these are given interest by huge climbing roses in white, one at least reaching almost to the top of its tree and at least thirty feet high.

Clematis are imaginatively used, but, in keeping with the simple cottage theme, there are no elaborate pergolas, most grown through shrubs or on wicker wigwams. I particularly loved the dark crimson blooms of *Clematis viticella* 'Royal Velours', contrasting with the grey leaves of the silver leaf pear *Pyrus salicifolia* 'Pendula'.

There is a smaller grassed area on the other side of the house, and here the lawn is cut into a spiral pattern, while more wide borders burst with colour. There are holly-hocks and roses against the walls, with great clumps of lavender threaded by the pink and white everlasting pea *Lathyrus latifolius*. In

this part of the garden yellow phlomis take the place of the anthemis, and the unusual white form of *Epilobium angustifolium f. albiflorum* — better known as fireweed — makes a tall background to *Alchemilla mollis*, dianthus and delphiniums.

There is a further sunken courtyard area approached by the steps that lead to the back door. It contains an old well, now boarded up and filled with red and pink pelargoniums in pots. The house wall plays host to a large fig, while purple sage, choisya and foxgloves fight for space. A magnolia on a single stem (the largest tree in the garden apart from the conifers on the periphery) shades the steps, while utilitarian objects such as dustbins are disguised by wicker covers.

The hamlet of Boningale contains many other distinguished timber buildings and a fascinating Norman church, but it is difficult to imagine a prettier picture than The Old Farmhouse and its garden. It is also worth mentioning that although the garden proper is small, there is a further eleven acres of field with pond, newly planted trees and wild flowers, in which to wander.

The Old Rectory • Rodington

A traditional country garden, with formal water features and an extensive wild flower area.

Open under the National Gardens Scheme, see Yellow Book

A house called The Old Rectory conjures up pictures of tea on the lawn on a hot, still, mid-summer's day. We visited in early July in just those conditions, the air warm and scented by roses, while the sounds of water splashing followed us from one part of the garden to another.

The house also fits into preconceived ideals, being an early Victorian (1840) building with an elegant frontal elevation, and tall windows overlooking the main garden. The garden was in fact designed to look good from the windows on this side, echoing the symmetrical layout of the house; the whole softened by a magnificent wisteria reaching to the roof and profuse planting in the herbaceous beds around the neatly mown grass.

The main plot, however, revolves around a spectacular fountain in the centre of the lawn. This consists of a large round pond with water-lilies and a tiered fountain, the whole emphasised by a walkway from the front of the house which goes on to encircle the water. I loved the way Victorian tile edging had been used to define the path. In fact, attention to detail is not the least of this garden's many charms.

The owners have lived at The Old Rectory for ten years, finding just a paddock when they came — although with some good trees, including an enormous Wellingtonia which must be contemporary with the house. Much manure was incorporated in the early stages, and, as the surrounding area is sandy, gave the new plantings a good start. They had only a little gardening knowledge, although there is a tradition of gardening lore on both sides of the family, and learned 'on the job'. I admired their lovely mix of foliage colours: red of cotinus, yellow from clipped privet, purple berberis, and every shade of green. So often in a large garden foliage is overlooked, but it adds much to the garden picture when flowers have faded.

The mixed beds around the central lawn were full of all the high summer favourites when we visited — delphiniums, campanulas, phlox, hardy geraniums and the gorgeous dark red *Knautia macedonica*, a unique colour, so good with blues and mauves. White notes came from dog daisies and phlox, while clematis added more soft blues, as well as glowing purple.

A pergola hung with wisteria, climbing roses and clematis runs alongside the main lawn behind the herbaceous borders. An urn

making a focal point at one end, whilst a wonderful group of day lilies marks the beginning of the walk. One of these I recognised as *Hemerocallis* 'Hyperion', a very good, clear yellow, but another smaller dark crimson, almost with a brown tinge, is of unknown variety as it was already growing in the garden when the owners moved in. There are now so many day lilies available, with new forms apparently being added every week, it is probably a good idea to pay little attention to names, so many being almost identical, and just buy them in flower from a reputable nursery.

Beyond the main lawn an arch leads into the wild garden, with mown paths through grass past the aforementioned Wellingtonia, and many mature trees. This area is under-planted with fritillaria, English bluebells and cowslips, making a perfect contrast to the more formal garden closer to the house. Other deft touches include three wicker sheep at the front of the house under a sumach tree, a metal heron, and a white terracotta dove perched on a tall pillar, for all the world as if it had just landed. I also thought the balls of clipped box growing in gravel together with large sculptural stones, all giving interest to a difficult shady area, a very clever idea. A sitting out paved garden close to the house contains a corner water feature; again, the sound and sight of water delightful on a hot afternoon.

Although only ten years old, this is a well-established and strongly designed garden, perfectly in keeping with the house it surrounds, but with enough freedom in the planting not to be dominated by its geometric layout.

Oteley · Ellesmere

A dramatic landscape garden of ten acres running down to the Mere, and containing many fascinating follies. Open under the National Gardens Scheme, see Yellow Book

Driving along the busy road that skirts the Mere at Ellesmere, one looks across a wide expanse of water towards a green vista of trees sweeping down to the lakeside. In the winter, when the leaves have fallen, tantalising glimpses of weathered sandstone are just visible, and I must surely not be the first person to wonder exactly what is on the other side. Many years ago I discovered that it was something rather special.

To begin with the setting, Oteley lies among the drumlins of north Shropshire, those humpy mounds of debris left by the retreating glaciers at the end of the last ice age. The melting ice was also responsible for the meres, creating the 'Shropshire Lake District' and giving Oteley its unique flavour. There have been several houses at Oteley. It is marked on Saxton's map of 1577 when it was a classic Shropshire black and white timber-framed house. This was replaced in 1827 by a large, neo-Elizabethan mansion with which the layout of the gardens are contemporary. Soon after the Second World War this in turn was demolished and replaced by a modern house.

The gardens are the work of many generations, and a previous owner terraced the sloping ground leading to the lake with imposing 'Gothic' grey sandstone walls and steps. Not content with this, he then proceeded to pave the level areas between the steps with grey and white pebbles laid in intricate patterns of circles and lines. The designs have a Celtic flavour, but are the work of craftsmen imported from Italy whose descendants, it is said, are still to be found in the village of Cockshutt.

The area now has a great deal more tree cover than was originally intended, but this, in my opinion, adds rather than detracts from the overall romantic picture. The stone walls are green with lichen and host to climbers such as wisteria, ivy and *Hydrangea petiolaris*, while the water appears suddenly and mysteriously down a flight of steep steps at the side of a stone boat house. There are cool, dark grottoes set into the walls, one with a wrought-iron window reminiscent of a Spanish balcony, while a bird's-eye panorama of paving, steps and the lake, is obtained from a viewing platform close to what looks like the remains of an ancient sundial.

A narrow path, overhung with rhododendron and acers casting dappled shadows, follows the edge of the water closely until one bursts out into the sunlight, sloping lawns and a landscape containing some of the most magnificent and imposing trees in the county. Rivalling the height of some of the tallest trees (not excepting venerable cedars and wellingtonias) is an extraordinary tower in red and grey sandstone, complete with metal weather vane and viewing balcony. The tall trees around help the enormous scale of this building to fit into the landscape, while the ivy and hydrangea with which the base is clothed tie it into the garden. I was reminded of Princess Rapunzel, who let down her hair from the top of just such a tower.

The specimen trees and shrubs in this area have all reached full maturity and include a superb Brewer's weeping spruce, *Acer palmatum* 'Dissectum', always tricky to

get to any size as it hates wind and late frosts, as well as quite the largest *Kalmia latifolia* that I have ever seen. The latter has fascinating pinky-white flowers like clusters of tiny lanterns, and needs acid soil and some shelter to thrive.

On the other side of a red sandstone wall pierced by an entrance complete with benches, and topped by a tiny room lit by a leaded window, is the 'Swiss Cottage'. This wonderful folly is now the abode of pigeons and other birds, but must have once given endless pleasure to generations of children who lived in the big house.

Large island beds are a feature in this part of the garden, again in keeping with the

grand scale, some containing trees and shrubs, others including tall perennials, and one devoted entirely to grasses. A particularly interesting sheltered corner is composed of blue-grey eucalyptus — some tall, some lopped — and dark lead cherubs, all set against a weathered brick wall which sports an extra large *Magnolia grandiflora*. The latter must be amazing in flower as it covers the very high wall from top to bottom. Undulating herbaceous borders follow this wall (on the other side of which is the vegetable plot) towards the house, where the whole garden becomes more formal.

This is a new house in an old setting, but the general layout has been retained, with many original outbuildings and walls. A well planned terrace gives views over the lawns, though trees hide the lake; while at the rear

of the house, a square courtyard has borders packed with interesting plants, mostly in shades of white in early June. These range from the difficult *Clematis armandii*, through the spectacular *Wisteria sinensis* in white, to the easy but beautiful *Anthemis cupaniana*. I also loved the olearia, a mass of white daisies, tree heathers and *Crambe cordifolia*. Another memory near the walled kitchen garden is a symphony in yellow, containing rubus, a yellow leaf acer, golden elm and a pale yellow ivy. I don't know whether any of this was ever planned on paper, but it certainly works.

How can on sum up this wonderful garden, perhaps as ten acres of sheer delight. My abiding thought is how much fun someone had in planning it, and how much pleasure it has continued to give succeeding generations over the years.

The Patch • Acton Pigot

A plant connoisseur's garden, containing National Collections of camassias, dictamnus and veratrum.

Open under the National Gardens Scheme, see Yellow Book

The description is in the name. The Patch is just a patch, but also a treasure ground of the rare and the beautiful. The owner (a founder member of the Shropshire branch of the National Council for the Conservation of Plants in Gardens) describes it as a conservation garden, and it does contain no less than three National Collections. The garden is planned to give interest all year round, and also plays host to an especially important collection of rare snowdrops and hellebores. We visited in early June, when the camassias in blue and white were almost over, but the dictamnus and veratrums took one's breath away.

Dictamnus, which look similar to stubby foxgloves, are a favourite of mine as they need little staking, appear to be subject to no diseases, and have a further, fascinating property — they give off a volatile oil which, it is said, one can set alight on a still, warm, evening. Neither I nor the owner of The Patch have ever tried it however!

Veratrums have the most extraordinary pleated leaves and greenish flowers. The leaves though are their *raison d'être*. They push out of the ground folded like a fan which slowly opens as the plant grows, and they do best in rich, moist soil and light shade, which they get in abundance at The Patch.

The National Collections are not the only treasures however. To start with the largest plants, several mature trees caught my eye. *Eucalyptus niphophila* has the smooth, fleshy trunk of the beech, but in shades of grey, beige and white. Hard to better, but nearby is *E. n.* 'de Beuzeville', whiter and even more sinuous. Eucalyptus are not all hardy (they are natives of Australia) but seed obtained from higher altitudes will produce plants which survive in all but the worst winters. Mention must also be made of *Sorbus aucuparia* in the golden leaf form. I love sorbus because I find them both easy and beautiful, but this graceful tree was completely new to me. *S. aucuparia* is, of course, our native Rowan, or mountain ash, and there are many different forms. It is an ideal tree for a small garden being abundant in flower and fruit, as well as sporting interesting leaves.

Moving lower down to shrub level it is hard to know where to begin. A combination that stood out is *Sambucus nigra* 'Black Beauty', a particularly dark leafed form of the common elder with pink flowers, planted next to an abies, or Silver Fir, with the most glorious, duck-egg blue new foliage. This conifer has an interesting history as it was purchased as a prostrate plant from a N.C.C.P.G. sale. The local rabbit population — with which the garden is plagued — immediately chewed off all the new growth and it metamorphosed into a vertical form. Looking at it now, I am sure the owner must be pleased that the rabbits had their way with this one.

These animals do pose a more serious problem when it comes to the herbaceous perennials, however, even causing the owner to give up her National Collection of epimediums. She copes by growing rabbit proof plants, or, if they are vulnerable in the early stages of growth, using collars of wire netting. Not pretty, but it does enable plants to get a start. I must say though, speaking from bitter experience, it is quite extraordinary what a small mesh baby rabbits can squeeze through.

The Patch is laid out with a maze of narrow paths, enabling one to get close to the herbaceous treasures and bulbs. There is a white garden, but plants are placed in positions that suit their habit of growth or cultivation requirements, rather than 'arranged' in any formal way.

I was drawn first to the boldly striped sisyrinchium *S. striatum* 'Variegatum', with pale, straw coloured, yellow flowers, because I cannot keep it in my own garden. It is apparently susceptible to late frosts, although has a plain leafed cousin that is almost a weed. The trilliums, also enjoying the moist, leafy shade, were especially good in 2003 and are inter-planted with ferns and hosta which like the same conditions. I noted the blue *Hosta* 'Halcyon', as well as a striking dark green form with a pure white edge to the leaf. Hostas are of course grown mostly for their foliage, but I enjoy the flowers too, which betray their relationship to the lily family. These are usually a subtle greeny/white or pale mauve, and blend in well with most colour schemes.

Numerous plants are allowed to self-seed at The Patch. Aquilegias are treated in this way, and I am sure hybridise promiscuously producing lots of different shapes and colours. A dark red, and another very dark purple and white, looked particularly eye catching, although the only named variety I definitely identified was the green cream and pink congested double, *Aquilegia* 'Nora Barlow'.

Iris are another speciality of the garden, as are paeonia and alliums. Among the latter is a superb dark purple *Allium aflatunense* 'Purple Sensation', as well as a group of *A. christophii*.

The previous garden made by the owner of The Patch featured on the cover of our first book *Some Shropshire Gardens*. I think she has created an even better one now.

Preen Manor • Church Preen

An outstanding garden of gardens covering six acres, sited on the remains of a Cluniac monastery.

Open under the National Gardens Scheme, see Yellow Book

The gardens at Preen Manor inhabit a site steeped in history. It began in the twelfth century with the establishment of a Cluniac cell as an outpost of Wenlock Priory; the church being constructed about one hundred years later. It is clearly visible from many points in the garden, especially the dramatic battlements of the later chapel. The old priory ruins at Preen were demolished in Victorian times, and the then fashionable architect Norman Shaw employed to terrace the gently sloping site and build a suitably impressive house. Sadly, it proved too grand to maintain and was razed to the ground in the 1920s. However, all was not lost as an enormous chimney and part of the ground floor remained; these were rebuilt into a charming house of more manageable size. In the gardens are many relics of the past, all incorporated into the design: the original terracing, wonderful trees (including the oldest yew in Shropshire supposedly planted in AD 457), a magnificent grey stone wall with brick buttressing, various sections of older walls, as well as monastic remains such as the monks' bathing pools, many of the latter hidden in the thick woods which surround the property.

A walk around the gardens at Preen Manor begins at the spectacular entrance, with the churchyard and grey stone porch before you, all enclosed by low, razor-sharp hedges. I very much admired the stone trough filled with white begonias, blue and white lobelia, and trailing pelargoniums. A gap in the trees allows views to distant hills, while buddlias in blues and mauves peep over one of the many walls in the garden. The whole site is conceived as a series of gardens in the style of Hidcote and

Sissinghurst, although to my eye the terracing with the huge cedar of Lebanon below, the massed rhododendrons and the long canal, remind me of Bodnant Gardens in north Wales. Even Bodnant, however, would be envious of the wonderful wall which runs along the slope and gives such character and structure to the main garden. This wall was part of Norman Shaw's original plan, and is buttressed along its entire length with orange-red brick. In the past it was covered with climbers, as the remains of old nails testify, but is now fronted by only a low yew hedge, square cut topiary decorating the lawn before it. Simplicity itself, but a perfect contrast to the busy fruit and vegetable garden behind.

This is the part of the garden in which we saw most change, as it had only just been laid out when we last visited fourteen years ago. Now the roses meet overhead on the iron arches which mark the paths, each radiating out like the spokes on a wheel from the central round bed of herbs closely confined by box hedging. Box is the main edging plant used, but espalier fruit trees also divide the plot, while standard gooseberries form edible full stops. There is another mini-orchard of dwarf fruit trees near by, sheltered by a yew hedge threaded with the blue of the trailing *Campanula garganica*.

The Chess Garden, complete with giant chess set, is part of a sunken area that was once a swimming pool but now sports a double line of dwarf conifers, namely *Chamaecyparis lawsoniana* 'Ellwood's Gold', which must be the ideal choice wherever a tightly elegant effect is required. Although the garden has many formal areas like this, there is no sense of 'over design'. Paths take

a natural course following the lie of the land, although all parts are clearly defined by walls and hedges. The severity of a plain rondel of hornbeam with a large Greek urn as a centrepiece, is set off by steps leading through banks of rough grass filled with wild flowers and early bulbs. Nearby, a stone lion sits at the end of a dead straight avenue, while an informal, shady nut walk leads to an iron seat; the borders under the hazels filled to overflowing with hardy geraniums and hosta.

Close to the greenhouses, and in a separate area laid out with cold frames, is perhaps the most perfect garden shed that we have yet encountered. 'Shed' is really too mundane a word to describe it, as it is built of brick with a clock over the door, a cockerel weather vane on top, and immaculately maintained inside, with neat shelves for pots, chemicals and other garden necessities. It provides one side of yet another small, enclosed plot, this time with stone-filled oblong pond, water trickling gently over a large rock at its centre. Here can be seen large pots containing the bright red dahlia 'Bishop of Llandaff', an excellent choice as the pots can be taken indoors, thereby saving oneself the chore of regularly lifting the tubers. More pots are placed on brick steps, and these contain an eclectic mixture of canna, agaves, grasses, ferns and arum lilies, all backed by a wall hung with Virginia creeper; which must be quite a sight in October.

Other memories include a bed of scented yellow lilies placed just below the kitchen window, a border of *Penstemon* 'Garnet', the hardiest of all the penstemons, and a dark purple leafed heuchera used as an edging in the rose garden. Borders around the beautiful grey stone house are mostly devoted to day lilies in yellow, white phlox, *Linaria* 'Canon Went' in soft pink, white flowered white variegated honesty (the very best kind *if* you can get it), deciduous blue ceanothus and campanulas, with white agapanthus to

come. I appreciated the way the border right across the lawn in front of the house had been kept low so as not to interrupt the view. In fact, the latter point is indicative of the thought and attention to detail inherent throughout the whole plot. Perfection whichever way one looks, with a rightness and naturalness somehow blending with formality and the unchanging, underlying bones of the garden.

Rowan Cottage • St Martins

A small plantswoman's garden created in 1997, full of unusual trees, shrubs and perennials.

Open annually for the Shropshire and Mid Wales Hospice — see local press for details

The garden at Rowan Cottage is small by any standards, and the owner can only be described as a plantaholic. Put the two together, and you will begin to understand why something rather extraordinary has been achieved. How can there be room for a winter garden, many big trees, shrubs large and small, uncountable herbaceous perennials, a comprehensive hardy geranium collection, pond, lawn — admittedly minute — patio and Spanish garden. I could go on, but will let you into some of the garden's secrets.

Firstly and most important, the owner gardens on no less than five distinct levels. The tall tree canopy with well defined trunks producing shady areas; shrubs mostly used as background to give privacy, although some are sympathetically pruned to fit in further forward; herbaceous perennials beautifully graded for height and spread; low growing alpines and edging plants used as ground cover and overflowing onto paths; and finally, early bulbs, in their full glory in the winter garden, and at their best of course before the main garden gets going.

The whole garden is so well planned that I am reminded of a vast flower arrangement, every single plant getting its fifteen minutes of fame before it is covered by a clematis or hidden by a neighbour whose time has come. Did I mention that there are over forty clematis in the garden? Whereas I walk around my own garden despairing over lack of wall or trellis, the owner of Rowan Cottage plants her climbers close to shrubs, and then lets them get on with it. It seems to work, although she does admit some losses.

Close packing equals much feeding, but the soil is naturally fertile, so a combination of Growmore pellets and mulching with manure is used in the winter. An interesting idea — as there is no room for a compost heap — is to compost 'on the spot' so to speak. All green rubbish and kitchen waste is chopped up, buried and then rots underground.

I saw Rowan Cottage several years ago in its early stages when it seemed rather

enclosed by other houses, but now the garden has matured, the many shrubs planted along its borders giving almost total privacy as well as shelter from strong winds. A superb variegated elder makes a good corner piece and has been left to grow to its full height, while the more refined *Sambucus nigra* 'Black Beauty' is regularly pruned hard to fit into a more conspicuous place. The owner is still adding plants and is on the look out for *S. n.* 'Black Lace', just as good a colour as 'Black Beauty' but with serrated leaves.

There is no fear of really big trees, in spite of the size of the garden. The owner states that they are to be preferred in a small plot, as one can cultivate right up to the trunk of a tall tree — the canopy is high and out of the way, creating places for plants that enjoy some protection from hot sunlight.

Herbaceous perennials range from the easy, like *Geranium phaeum* in several forms — a great plant for deep shade — to the outstandingly rare and choice. The latter includes a wonderful clear blue penstemon grown close to *Artemisia* 'Limelight'. The latter is a variegated form which looks as if it ought to be tender, but thrives at Rowan Cottage. I coveted the monkshood, *Aconitum* 'Stainless Steel', a very descriptive name as it perfectly describes the subtle colour of this outstanding plant. Also noted were a tricyrtis with a gold leaf, and a *Geranium* 'Thurstonianum' with a tiny pink flower instead of the usual mauve.

The Spanish garden, newly created in 2004 from an old outbuilding with its roof removed, has painted yellow walls and a sitting out place. In a pot is a fabulous foliage plant — *Rhamnus frangula* 'Asplenifolia', grown chiefly for its thread-like leaves, but also covered in tiny perfumed flowers, the scent enhanced and intensified by the garden walls. I think that if I had to pick just one shrub to take home with me, however, it would be the *Neillia*

thibetica with its drooping pink racemes of flowers and buds.

One hardly notices the fences surrounding the garden, now completely hidden by shrubs and climbers, but within the garden proper escallonia is used as a division. It is a glossy evergreen and can be clipped right back many times a year to keep it compact and neat. Then there's the garage wall, once an eyesore, but now covered in a variegated ivy so that it provides a green and yellow background for the pond.

If you are about to plan or alter a small garden, don't miss Rowan Cottage — you will rarely see a better example of 'how to do it'.

Ruthall Manor • Ditton Prors

A medium sized country garden with rare trees, an old horse pond, and many unusual perennials.

Open under the National Gardens Scheme, see Yellow Book

After describing the thirty-foot high Mimosa at Belle Vue Road in Shrewsbury as the most amazing horticultural sight in Shropshire, it was perhaps inevitable that I should — the very next month — be confronted by another equally remarkable. This time a mature *Paulownia fargesii* in full flower. This superb tree has only flowered really well three times during its entire lifetime, being a martyr to the April frosts to which our climate is particularly prone and which destroy the flower buds. To see a forest-sized tree hung with large, mauvy-blue, foxglove-shaped bells, is an experience I wouldn't have missed for the world. The problem is in finding a planting position, for it needs a sheltered, well-drained site in full sun, and the flowers can be lost against a blue sky. At Ruthall Manor the background is dark green, which shows off the blooms (sometimes described as heliotrope) to perfection.

Ruthall Manor has changed little since it featured in our first book on Shropshire gardens, although the complicated layout planned by its garden designer owner (now retired) has obviously matured over a decade, with many of the trees now at their best. The horse pond continues to be a delight, with candelabra primula, iris and ferns blending into a harmonious whole. The weeping lime at its edge is much bigger, but still provides essential shelter from its acid green leaves, although it now requires regular pruning to allow a passage under its branches.

Ruthall Manor was mentioned in the Domesday Book, but the house is Georgian, whilst the whole complex of farm buildings somehow exude a distinctly Victorian feel. The garden revolves around the main building with the front overlooking a long lawn bordered by paths, trees, shrubs and herbaceous perennials. A new innovation at the end of the lawn is a gravelled sculpture garden inspired by two old conifers which had become too large, and which have been cut down to just their multi-stemmed trunks, thus providing an impressive pillared entrance. Most of the sculptures are ceramic, but there are also a number of iron pieces throughout the garden.

Close to the house is a paved area with a sunny sitting out place, again with well-designed iron seats. I loved the use made of choisya, or Mexican orange blossom, one in

the yellow-leafed form, one plain green, on each side of the path and giving fragrance and flowers as well as interesting leaf shape throughout the year.

I always admired the choice of trees at Ruthall Manor and was fascinated to see in just one glade nearly all my favourites, including *Betula albo-sinensis septentrionalis* with its tattered bronze bark and an unusual grey 'bloom' to the whole trunk; *Acer griseum*, the paperbark maple, the very best choice for a small garden, with scarlet autumn leaves and flaking, curling bark; also a variegated tulip tree and *Acer cappadocicum* 'Aureum', the latter having red new growth and golden-yellow mature leaves. The under-planting is *Euphorbia robbiae* and bergenia, both ideal for a dry, difficult situation in fairly deep shade.

Back in the main garden I noted several unusual shrubs all doing well, including an extraordinary *Paeonia suffruticosa*, or tree peony, with white, double flowers the size of dinner plates. These old hybrids, although sometimes difficult to get going and expensive to buy, repay their keep many times over by being very long lived and flowering well year after year. There is also an unusual holly in this part of the garden, *Ilex* 'Ferox Aurea', the variegated form of the hedgehog holly, so called because it has spines on the surface of the leaf as well as the edges. It is slow growing, and for those who like curiosities, is believed to be one of the oldest identifiable hollies still in cultivation. Other good ones recommended by the owner of Ruthall Manor are 'Milk Boy', 'Dairy Maid' and 'Handsworth New Silver'. The latter I once grew and loved myself; it has purple stems and the most attractive green leaves with a wide cream edge.

Everything seems to do well at Ruthall Manor, and beneath the hollies are drifts of lily-of-the-valley, while the primula overflow from their rightful place beside the pond and have to be weeded out of paths. The weed bitter cress also has to be dug out frequently,

but the lily-of-the-valley and the primula are winning the battle. A labour intensive garden like Ruthall is not easy to maintain, but the owner manages with just a little help a few times a week, finding that most of her problems come from plants which like the place too well and are inclined to 'get away'. I agree that there are some plants it is very tricky to have just a little of, and that they are perhaps best avoided, no matter how beautiful.

Trees of course play the major role in this lovely garden, but the pond, perennials, sculpture and shrubs make it enjoyable in any season of the year.

Scotsman's Field • Church Stretton

A large Edwardian house and garden designed by Sir Ernest Newton.

Open under the National Gardens Scheme, see Yellow Book

Having already visited an 'Arts and Craft' house at Adcote (see page 12) whose architect was Norman Shaw, it was interesting to view the house and garden at Scotsman's Field designed by Ernest Newton, one of his pupils. Based on an E-plan, it was built in 1908, and is a large house with gables sporting typical, Ernest Newton metal-faced bay windows over-looking the terrace leading down to the gardens. The house (now divided sympathetically into three separate dwellings) and garden are a rare survival from the Edwardian age, a period which seems undervalued in comparison with Elizabethan or Georgian architecture, and offers a fascinating glimpse into a vanished age only just passing from living memory.

The house stands at the top of a steep slope with a south-eastern aspect, and it was the centre portion — which claims the major part of the garden — which engaged our attention. The architect believed that the garden is an essential component in the design of a house, and the layout is contemporary with the original building, the 1960 sub-divisions following the old walls and hedges so that the basic structure remains as it was in 1908.

The owners have lived in the house since 1977 and see themselves rather as custodians of the property and gardens, so that any changes have been of a minor nature. Interesting components of the garden are the great grassy banks, which are now used as miniature sloping wild-flower and bulb meadows, but were once meticulously mown. This seems an excellent way to keep the original spirit of the concept, while adapting it to modern life where there is less time — and fewer gardeners — to deal with the difficult slopes.

The upper part of the bank boasts an impressive flight of steps which divide half way down, making for a dramatic entrance. The whole effect, however, is softened by self-sown sedums. At the bottom of the steps is a large rectangular lawn, ideal for Edwardian pursuits such as tennis or croquet, surrounded by clipped yew hedges. The owners experimented with a long beech hedge to divide the lawn from the terrace and break the garden up, so that all could not be viewed at once. However, the hedge proved too heavy and dense and has been replaced by a beautiful iron-work screen which follows the Arts and Craft pattern on the porch. This now plays host to a collection of clematis in many shades of mauve and purple. There is just enough cover to give interest, without hiding the intricacies of the iron-work; always a tricky feat.

To the right and left of the steps are two magnificent herbaceous borders in contrasting hot and cool colours. The hot border contains no pink, but at the time we visited in late summer sported day lilies, orange helenium, *Crocosmia* 'Lucifer', inula, a gorgeous pale cream potentilla and phlox, as well as many orange and apricot crocosmia still to come. The owners also make use of small dahlias in suitable colours, supposedly tender, but left to take their chance all winter. The garden is six hundred feet up, but the steep slope allows frost to roll away and the soil is a free draining loam.

The cool border, divided from the hot border by a conservatory in the space between the steps, contains no yellow and was full of white phlox, *Verbena bonariensis*, poppies, purple hardy geranium, *Eryngium giganteum* 'Miss Willmott's Ghost', Joe Pye weed and more pom-pom dahlias, as well as *Clematis integrifolia* grown from seed.

The garden lies in the shelter of the Church Stretton hills, surrounded by woods and fields and is therefore a Mecca for wildlife. Badgers appear regularly in the evening, and I don't think that I have ever spotted so many butterflies all together, clustered around a variegated buddleia with glorious dark purple flowers. This form is a definite improvement on the weak *Buddleia* 'Variegata', or *B.* 'Harlequin', which has washed out pink-purple flowers.

Beyond the large lawn the garden slopes further into a wilder, shady area full of fruit trees used as props for vigorous roses such as 'Paul's Himalayan Musk' and 'Bobbie James'. Here the owners grow some real treasures such as *Arisaema ringens* and *A.*

speciosum, with an enormous single leaf. Arisaema are a large genus related to the arum lily, with pitcher-like flowers not unlike our native lords and ladies. Some of the rarer forms have interesting striped markings and all appreciate cool, woodland conditions. Other very unusual plants in this part of the garden include a hogweed, *Heracleum* 'Washington Lime', with vibrant yellow new growth. Heracleums are not for the faint hearted, growing six to eight feet high, but are striking plants for the back of the border, and are generally trouble free.

One of the owners of Scotsman's Field is a botanical artist, so colour combinations throughout the garden are chosen with a painter's eye. I especially admired the subtle combination of *Clematis orientalis* 'Bill Mackenzie' with a golden hop. Altogether a wonderful garden, full of historical and botanical interest, fortunate to have fallen into the hands of such knowledgeable and devoted owners.

The Shear • Nash

A large, well-stocked garden around a fifteenth-century farmhouse, with extensive views.

Open under the National Gardens Scheme, see Yellow Book

The house at The Shear has stood since the fifteenth century, whilst the garden was created in the last twenty years, but it blends into its surroundings as effortlessly as does the building. This is a country garden *par excellence*, and I loved every inch of it: the overflowing beds full of healthy plants, all nourished on a rich diet of horse and sheep manure; the wonderful house, with lichen covered grey stone walls hung with roses and clematis; the stupendous views over rolling Shropshire hills, and the final perfect touch of white doves circling against a blue sky.

The owners found very little when they moved in in 1986 and have gradually expanded to create a garden which is a fascinating mixture of the formal and the informal. The front of the house faces south, and retains the ancient cobbled path to the front door with herbaceous perennials on each side. There are many old favourites: oriental poppies, delphiniums and paeonia, as well as some very tender shrubs such as fatsia, which I was amazed to see growing out of doors in cold, inland Shropshire. Also

on the south side I noticed pittosporum, piptanthus and crinodendron, all designated as distinctly 'tender' in most gardening books. On the building itself is an abutilon I would consider a house plant, as well as an enormous *Rosa* 'Mutabilis', trained against the wall. This rose is generally grown as a lax shrub and is usually bitten back by winter frosts, but at The Shear has reached the upper windows.

The flower-bordered path and uneven sloping lawn to the front of the house contrast with the more 'designed' garden at the side. This is reached by a well placed brick and wood pergola hung with a magnificent specimen of *Rosa* 'Climbing Cecile Brunner', the perfect pink miniature buttonhole rose, and, in my opinion, one of the top ten roses anyone can grow. Looking back down the pergola, a white dovecote makes a focal point across the lawn, where the birds bill and coo.

The owner has a penchant for circles and most of the beds in this part of the garden are round. I particularly admired a circular

construction with an urn as a centrepiece, quartered by stone paths. The soil is completely hidden by dianthus and the compact sanguineum geraniums in various forms, including the white *Geranium sanguineum album*, pink *G. s. var. lancastriense*, and the more common cerise colour. In fact the garden abounds with all the best hardy geraniums, including the tiny *G. robertianum* 'Celtic White' and the dark purple *G. psilostemon*, as well as the not to be missed *G. pratense* 'Plenum Caeruleum', a truly superb double. Another circular, sunken garden is devoted to hybrid tea roses confined by box hedges.

Close to the house a raised bed topped by a gravel mulch is full of small treasures, an ideal way to grow alpines which will not stand the heavy clay soil at The Shear. Nearby, a pot garden stands in a shady corner and includes a fair sized mimosa in full flower. (Mine refuses to produce a single bud!) Roses on this side of the house are 'Maigold', 'Queen Elizabeth' and 'Madame Isaac Pereire', as well as a *Magnolia grandiflora*. The latter is not to be attempted unless you have a really sheltered place against a warm wall.

I was intrigued by a group of hydrangeas in a low part of the garden prone to damp. I have always found hydrangeas difficult to grow successfully in Shropshire, as foliage and buds seem to be pinched by cold in all but the mildest winters. Again, the favourable micro-climate at The Shear was proved by the healthy looking new growth covering the plants.

Also in this area I noted an unusual tree newly planted — *Alnus glutinosa* 'Imperialis', with deeply cut, ferny leaves, unlike any alder I have ever seen before. This tree grows in company with willows planted to suck up excessive moisture, a trick I have also found useful. Other trees in dryer parts of the plot are under-planted with different varieties of lavender. It should not thrive in heavy clay soil, liking dry, sandy conditions, but I can only say the ones at The Shear looked very happy to me.

All parts of the garden flow effortlessly one into another, tied together by self-sown foxgloves. (The purple kind are ruthlessly pulled up, to encourage the white and peach ones to seed) Even the wilder garden beyond the main plot is sympathetically planted to harmonise with the garden proper.

I loved every inch, from the superb *Clematis tangutica* on the stable at the back of the house, flowering at least a month early, to the magical setting in one of the most beautiful and still unspoilt parts of Shropshire. I am sure I wasn't the first nor the last on which this garden has left a lasting memory.

Swallow Hayes • Albrighton

A large, well-stocked garden containing the National Collections of hamamelis and Russell lupins.

Open under the National Gardens Scheme, see Yellow Book

Visitors to our old garden at Erway Farmhouse often commented, with a hint of envy, that it must be wonderful to have your very own unlimited source of plants. (We had a tiny nursery). The owner of Swallow Hayes and her husband were developing a well known plant centre at the time their garden was being planned, so really did have that much desired, inexhaustible supply. The end result is a large, well-stocked garden, filled with the rare and the choice.

It was designed in the late sixties from a flat field, with several aims in mind. Firstly, as a personal and private garden, then as a stock bed to provide cuttings for the nursery, and lastly as a home for the National Collections of hamamelis or witch hazel, and Russell lupins. When we visited in late May, the Russell lupins — which inhabit a trial plot to themselves away from the main garden — were a sight to behold, their columns of colour clashing and harmonising above a sea of green leaves. Russell lupins are raised from seed, and rogue plants — those where you can see the stem, of indifferent colour, or just weak — must be ruthlessly culled. When a good plant is selected it is named, and thereafter propagated by cuttings. The hamamelis of course come into their own in February, or even as early as January in a good year, and can be found in the Winter Garden along with other spring bulbs, perennials and shrubs.

Swallow Hayes covers two acres, and considering that it has only been in existence for just over thirty years, has a very mature and settled air. This is chiefly because of the many tall, fully grown trees,

some — a *Metasequoia glyptostroboides* in particular — of such height and spread, that it is difficult to believe they were only planted in 1968. As well as an extensive collection of conifers, there are also many flowering cherries; one, a huge weeping *Prunus* 'Shidare-yoshino', covers a path and has to be pruned in the shape of a tunnel. Cherries of course are not very long lived, but any which deteriorate or die are used as supports for climbers, as are many other trees in the garden — the metasequoia for example sporting an enormous wisteria.

There are many choice magnolias to be seen, including the difficult *Magnolia campbellii* — its flowers tend to be affected by late frosts — which has just bloomed for the first time after a twenty year wait. I was intrigued by the cedar which grows in the rock garden, and which is heavily pruned every April to prevent it shading out the plants at its feet. This is a very 'Japanese' road to take, but it works well, the tree now fitting its allotted position. I also admired the little grotto nearby, originally planned to hide the plastic tunnel which covers the swimming pool, but having been carefully constructed of old weathered stone, now a focal point in its own right.

The garden is full of lime-hating plants, as the soil is a neutral light loam, including a collection of superb rhododendron. There are just too many choice plants to mention individually, but I was particularly taken by the huge yakushimanum hybrids, and a very striking 'hose in hose' double azalea in a glowing coral colour, called 'Norma'. ('Hose in hose' refers to one flower growing directly out of another, whilst 'doubling' means lots of petals radiating out from a central point.) The rhododendrons are mostly grown in large island beds, well shaded by a big weeping willow and many unusual birch trees. One group of the latter comprised *Betula nigra*, the river birch, with strange, shaggy bark; *B. pendula* 'Youngii', a dome-shaped weeping form, as well as many giant examples of the common type; again, each with its own attendant climber. In another bed a tall foxglove tree, *Paulownia tomentosa*, in glorious flower, provides exotic shade for yet more rhododendrons and azaleas.

I was pleased to make the acquaintance of the *Colletia armata* once more — it was an eight foot high bush when we last visited — but is now more like a small tree. This rarity from South America, with vicious spines and white flowers smelling of custard, is considered tender, but survives and flour-ishes at Swallow Hayes. In contrast, the owner is a hardy geranium aficianardo, and the garden is filled with these accommodating flowers, as well as favourite lupins from the trial garden, herbaceous peonies and iris.

Ferns are not forgotten, sited in the lower, damper sections of the plot — the whole area slopes gently away from the house — and revelling in an old, shaded, stone bordered well — really just a shallow depression in the ground — but perfect for ferns. There are a series of colour-coded small plots in this part of the garden, including a purple corner with dark red leafed shrubs and a grey area. Nearby is a large walnut tree under-planted with herbaceous perennials, thereby making nonsense of the rumour that nothing will grow under a walnut.

There is a weeping Judas tree, a plant that I have never encountered before, even in a botanical garden. In fact, with over three thousand plants in the garden, it would probably be easier to make a list of what isn't there!

All this is meticulously maintained with just a little help on one day a week, though the original design did have ease of maintenance as a priority in the plan. The garden is well sheltered by a leylandii hedge and its mature shrubs and trees, so there are few views out. In one part however, a laburnum tunnel (once just an arch) was constructed, and visitors look down a long grass path bordered by more plants to The Wrekin.

There is a small vegetable plot in the centre of the garden, and one constantly meets hidden, secret places around corners, or behind great banks of rhododendrons. This garden is a real *tour de force*, now at its mature best, and is an object lesson in how to turn a featureless field around a modern house into something both beautiful and characterful.

Acer Griseum grown for its wonderful tattered bark

Walcot Hall · Lydbury North

An outstanding country house rebuilt for Lord Clive of India, with an arboretum of national importance.

Open under the National Gardens Scheme, see Yellow Book

Approaching Walcot Hall an avenue of great oaks leads to an equally fine avenue of lime trees. This sets the scene for the whole garden which boasts some of the most magnificent trees, not only in Shropshire, but in the whole United Kingdom. Perhaps the *pièce de resistance* is the giant Douglas fir with a girth of twenty feet, one of a group raised from the original seed brought to this country by Douglas in 1827 and often described as the best in England. Other majestic specimens dotting the park include monkey puzzles, *Araucaria araucana*; larch in variety; the eastern hemlock, *Tsuga canadensis*; as well as all the cedars: *Cedrus libani*, the cedar of Lebanon; the Atlas cedar, *C. atlantica*; and the graceful *C. deodara*. The cedars in particular are a wonderful sight in late spring when pale new growth colours the leaves, their wide spreading branches overhanging the no less splendid rhododendrons and azaleas, which have also grown to tremendous proportions in their shade.

My other overall impression when visiting Walcot is of walls, both long and high, all built of brick in a subtle orange-red, and mostly covered in climbers, including quite the largest and most floriferous *Clematis montana* that I have ever seen. Not content with just a huge wall, this plant has climbed a tree and a house, and is now making its way along a wire support. All the walls protect and encircle the great house with its attendant stable block, again built of muted red brick with the exception of an imposing portico of grey stone Tuscan columns. The stableyard architecture is enlivened by a series of blank arches, an entrance decorated with more clematis, and a white painted lantern above.

The name Walcot derives from the Saxon for 'dwelling in the forest', and the house was rebuilt in its present form in 1763 by order of Lord Clive of India, who employed Sir William Chambers as his architect. At around the same time, a mile long serpentine lake was created at the front of the main building, so that a vista over water to the Long Mynd could be enjoyed from the principal rooms. Everything at Walcot appears to be on a grand scale: house, outbuildings, walls, shrubs and trees; but, because it has remained in private hands, the atmosphere is still that of a comfortable family house, albeit a country house with grounds bigger than most public parks. Walcot is also a garden of surprises, from the circular dovecote patronised not only by doves but a flock of chickens, to an extraordinary 'Russian style' church hidden deep in the woods, complete with copper domes, wood tiled roof and pointed steeple.

From the more formal garden close to the house, one climbs steep steps to the arboretum which rises from the rear of the main building. It is an amazing place, not a wood with rhododendrons but a rhododendron wood. Many are of great age, towering overhead and making gloomy tunnels which expose their sinuous, twisted trunks. The colours are dazzling in bright sunshine, from the usual pinks and mauves, to exotic whites with black and cream blotches, then darker, port-wine purples. This changes, as visitors make their way back down the hill, to the brilliant yellow, coral and peach of the azaleas; all signalling their presence by a heady perfume drifting through the trees. At one point, dark green water makes a clearing and serves as a mirror for purple clumps of

Rhododendrons and azaleas *en masse*

Rhododendron ponticum. This is how rhododendrons should be grown, with no restraints and surrounded by greenery in the shape of rare and native trees. It is of course all man-made, but nature has had her way for so long that, from the carpet of bluebells underfoot to the exotic conifers piercing the sky, it somehow appears perfectly natural.

There is a kitchen garden with greenhouse and flower-bordered walks between clipped box hedges, an iron pergola newly planted with alternate espalier apples and roses in the main garden, and a summer border set against yet another enormous wall. There is also the largest, longest and highest wisteria that I have ever encountered. Trees are still being planted in both arboretum and the garden proper; I noted a lovely Judas tree, *Cercis siliquastrum*, in full flower; a Brewer's weeping spruce, *Picea brewerana*, a breathtaking sight with its curtain-like branches, and several unusual sorbus.

It is a wonderful experience to visit this important and unique house in its splendid grounds at any time of the year, but when the rhododendrons and azaleas add their colour and scent, it can only be described as 'a knockout'.

The Watermill · Maesbrook

An old water mill dating from the seventeen-twenties, with a two acre garden designed to resist constant flooding. Open under the National Gardens Scheme, see Yellow Book

If one lives in a house called The Watermill sited on the Morda Brook just where it runs into the River Vyrnwy, one must expect the occasional flood. In the last decade the floods have been more than just an occasional blip so, wisely, the garden at The Watermill is designed to withstand repeated water logging. Fortunately the soil is a swiftly draining silt — the owners state that one can walk on it the day following a major flood. So — when the inevitable happens and the Severn is full, causing the Vyrnwy to rise and consequently the Morda Brook to overflow, with the result that The Watermill garden resembles a lake — all is not lost.

The site is in fact almost an island, forming a rough triangle with the Morda Brook and the Vyrnwy on two sides, the third channel consisting of a man-made canal. This is dry, excepting when the rivers are in flood, and used in the past as an overflow for the Morda Brook, diverting it so that repairs could be carried out on the great wheel that once drove the mill machinery. Milling ceased in the late nineteenth century with the decline of corn growing in the district, and after a disastrous fire destroyed the wheel. There is evidence of much activity in the distant past however, with bread ovens (they obviously baked as well as ground the corn) outbuildings, causeways across the river (still in view during a prolonged drought) and enormous flood protection banks called in Welsh 'argaes', which cover the ground for miles around.

When the owners moved in around 1998 they were faced with a difficult and challenging task, but with all the advantages that water in abundance and beautiful countryside around can bring to the general ambience of a garden. The whole area covers approximately two acres, and the portion close to the mill was tackled first, the remaining ground being used for grazing. There is an oblong herb garden, raised beds full of late summer perennials such as globe thistles and sedum, as well as a flight of steps to the top of the *argae* where one can look down at the Morda Brook running in a deep channel, and across to the main garden on the opposite bank. The sound of rushing water follows one around as it pours through two arches after running in a tunnel beneath the house, and it was fascinating to learn that the first intimation that floods are coming is complete silence, as the waterfalls are gradually overwhelmed by the rising water.

Informality is the keynote throughout the rest of the garden, with steep banks down to the river covered in wild flowers, including great stands of the Indian or Himalayan balsam, *Impatiens glandulifera*. This is a tall, pink flowered plant, introduced from the east in the early nineteenth century, and growing up to eight feet high in one season. It is regarded as a menace in some parts of the country where it has colonised every river bank with its popping, water-borne seeds, shading out native species. At The Watermill, this 'weed' looks very beautiful *en masse*, but one can have too much of a good thing! The owners cut great swathes down in late summer so that visitors can actually see the water, and burn the residue in the autumn when it has — hopefully — dried out.

The chief trees in the garden are not surprisingly willows, but many ornamental cherries were planted when the owners first moved in, and the old hazels which overhang the dry canal are a sight to behold, twisted and contorted into wonderful shapes. The owners are left with much wood — sleepers, branches and sometimes even whole trees — which are washed down and deposited after each flood, so have used some to construct a Victorian stumpery alongside the ditch, as well as covering the ground with blue-grey Welsh slates to make a pathway. Sleepers confine the small vegetable garden, making several raised beds to provide a rotation. There are many bulbs in the garden, including the semi-wild Tenby daffodil, *Fritillaria meleagris* and snowdrops, all of which withstand the constant water logging well. Further from the steep stone cladding close to the millrace, the gentle grassy banks of the Morda Brook were covered when we visited in late summer by the bright orange of crocosmia and the pink of polygonum.

Above the brook, near the apex of the triangular site and with a wonderful view of the distant Rodney's Pillar and the Llanymynech Hills across the point where the two rivers meet, a most original series of borders has been constructed. They are based on a circle, echoing the now long lost mill wheel, with a round grass centre, and six radiating triangular beds like slices of cake, each packed with flowers and shrubs of the hardiest, toughest kind. The backbone of the borders are dogwoods, both variegated and plain, but phlox, bronze fennel, lysimachia, sedums, *Rosa glauca*, rugosa roses, yellow rudbeckias and day lilies all seem to positively enjoy the occasional drenching with no adverse effects.

This garden must produce many agonising moments as precious plants are washed away, while new and exotic weeds spring up from seeds newly deposited by the river. But as the owners described the evening light reflected in the water, and the great flocks of birds which arrive when the river is 'up', as well as pointing out a tunnel where otters produced a litter last year, I couldn't help feeling that it was well worth the time and trouble.

Weston Park · Shifnal

A classic Restoration house surrounded by landscaped parkland and newly refurbished formal gardens.

Open frequently in season, please telephone: 01952 852100 for details

The Weston Park Estate straddles the border between Shropshire and Staffordshire. Indeed, from the semicircular Plane Tree Lawn, elegantly separated from the park by a stone balustrade, glimpses of The Wrekin are visible through gaps in the trees. Little is known of the origins of Weston, excepting that there was an 'upper' and 'lower' park in the seventeenth century intended for deer. The present dignified, symmetrical Restoration house is an important example of this style, and is constructed of mellow brick with stone details quarried locally at Tong Knoll. It sits in the centre of a superb park landscaped by Lancelot (Capability) Brown.

After Sir Henry Bridgeman inherited the estate in 1763, Brown's first task was to create a ha-ha on the south side of the house to separate the gardens from the parkland. (He later extended it to include Temple Wood, and was even commissioned to 'lower a hill'.) The Temple of Diana was constructed at about the same time, although it is in fact more of an orangery; it is built entirely of grey stone, with fierce, somewhat Islamic looking lions guarding the steps up to the wide glass doors. The only colour outside comes from a circular bed of vibrant red nasturtiums. James Paine, the architect, was responsible for the Roman Bridge which crosses a stream later dammed to create the Temple Pool. Much planting was carried out in the nineteenth century, although some of Capability Brown's original trees still remain, notably the magnificent sweet chestnuts with their dark, twisted, striated bark, and a large cedar.

The outbuildings at Weston include a genuine Victorian orangery and conservatory, the vast stableblock, a walled vegetable garden of five acres, as well as St. Andrew's church, and have been described in the past as 'like a village in itself'. The church is close to the house and clearly visible from the main garden. It has an early fourteenth-century tower, and contains some ancient wooden effigies of the Weston family.

The main flower garden is laid out on the south side of the house — once the main entrance — and is on two levels. It was redesigned in 1991, and now consists of a complicated formal garden in Victorian style, filled with bedding plants beautifully co-ordinated to blend and contrast. Close to the doors of the house, white Versailles tubs planted up with standard clipped evergreen trees at least eight feet high produce just the right formal note. The second level, reached by a flight of stone steps, is designed as a rose garden with dwarf box hedging. The white of the tubs is picked up by 'Iceberg' roses, while the pink standard rose trees are under-planted with *Stachys lanata*, or lamb's lugs. I loved the beds of closely planted heuchera, as well as the punctuation marks of clipped box, all echoed by corner pieces of neat, rounded, yellow privet bushes set in a perfect green lawn. The central focal point is a very large, stone, Victorian jardiniere, imaginatively planted with phormium and gypsophila. Only a container of this size could cope with such a combination, but how good it looked in the summer sunshine.

The Long Border contains an eclectic mixture of plants as diverse as day lilies, sedum, *Alchemilla mollis*, berberis in the form 'Rose Glow', *Penstemon* 'Garnet' in dark crimson, rue, dahlias and pink cistus. Low plants to the fore include euonymus and the curry plant, while the rounds of clipped box outlined by santolina, underline the strictly formal note.

On another side of the house is an Elizabethan parterre, known as the Italian Broderie Garden, and intended to be viewed from the Victorian orangery. Here again the dwarf hedges are of box, softened by the misty blue of nepeta and the grey of santolina. There are steps, neatly raked gravel, and a cherub fountain, all with a dramatic backdrop of church, house and impressive trees: copper beech, sweet chestnuts and lime. Colour comes from the yellow of *Hypericum* 'Hidcote' contrasting with the blue of buddlias, while bright red pelargoniums fill grey stone urns. Further on, more flashes of colour can be glimpsed in the conservatory, and the scented Rose Walk border is divided by clipped yew, to create separate areas for standard roses and banks of lavender.

Away from the great house, open doors in high walls lead one from sun to shade, while low flying swallows dive bomb visitors

and ducks make long V-shaped rills in the mirror-like water of the Church Pool. Maintenance is immaculate throughout the whole garden and park, but is especially impressive in this part, with sharply cut hedges, beautifully mown grass, and not a weed in sight. Around the Church Pool, edges are packed with gunnera, hydrangeas, bull-rushes (right in the water) and pink astilbe, not to mention willows, alders and a *Metasequoia glyptostroboides*.

Other delights at Weston Park, include more follies, such as the pink cottage, a tower, the boat house and Pendrell's cave.

The latter once housed a real hermit at a time when no self-respecting stately home could be without one.

I was impressed by the way all the children's entertainments, such as a full sized adventure playground and miniature railway, are sympathetically blended in well away from the main house so that they do not intrude on the peaceful ambience of the gardens.

Altogether a wonderful combination of architecture, glorious countryside, and formal, colourful gardens, giving visitors a glimpse back in time to a more unhurried, gentler age.

Wollerton Old Hall • Near Hodnet

A beautifully designed garden of gardens covering four acres centred on a sixteenth-century house.

Open Fridays and Sundays in season, as well as for the National Gardens Scheme.

See Yellow Book, or telephone: 01630 685760 for details

Wollerton Old Hall is not a single garden, but a whole series designed around a black and white Tudor manor house built in 1530. In the sixteenth century the wealthy elite favoured a formal, Flemish style, and this is chiefly what has been meticulously reproduced in the main garden at Wollerton, though using a far wider range of plants than was available in the past. Wollerton featured in our first book on Shropshire gardens, and we were fortunate to see it in its very early stages. Much has changed in fourteen years, though the 'bones' of the garden in the shape of walls, hedges and trees, do follow the basic pattern discernible in the late 1980s. The house and its outbuildings are an important element in the design, with various vistas and the main axis radiating out from the rear of the house. Formality is the keynote, with straight, ordered lines and tight, sharp cornered hedges enclosing each separate area. Every garden has its own theme and character, and this one is planned to perfection: not a vista without its focal point, or gateway without a pair of matching urns or further viewpoint leading one on.

There are no less than nineteen separate gardens, borders and walks defined within the whole area, but perhaps the part which has seen most change in the last fourteen years is the first portion visitors see between the house and the road, and which had yet to be developed in 1989. It now consists of a curved path with undulating borders and specimen trees set in immaculate green lawns. The house is a gem, and has been sympathetically restored, even to the extent of rebuilding a once demolished wing on the still existing sixteenth-century floor. There is also a totally new — to me — Croft, or wild area, outside the garden proper, with more specimen trees and wild flowers.

The 'garden' was a featureless field when the owners took over the property in 1984, though there were some good, mellow brick walls, and four old yew trees. The design was carefully worked out on paper, though trial and error also featured. The old garden close to the house, for example, which was the site of an Elizabethan knot garden, had to be altered as the box hedging developed a disease and is now a simple green garden very much in keeping with the house, consisting of Portuguese laurel edging a stone flagged path.

The sound of running water leads one to the Rill Garden which features a long canal on two levels with a central, square pond. Colours here are pale, with the pink of old roses picked up in the clumps of *Iris kaempferi* growing in each corner of the pool. I very much admired the use of weathered, grey oak fencing, echoing the use of wood on the house, all in 'Gothic' style, which divides the gardens or defines the borders. The same timber is used in the summer house, or gazebo, which overlooks the Rill Garden, and where one can sit and admire whilst enjoying the scent of the white climbing rose almost hiding the roof.

A change from formality can be found close by in the Shade Garden, where dry shade is exploited to grow ferns, hellebores and bulbs; all at their best in early spring. The main herbaceous border must be at least twelve feet deep, and is a *tour de force* in high summer. It has the classic backing of a high wall and owes much to Gertrude Jekyll's principles of colour co-ordination — that is shades based on the colour-wheel of warm through to cool, running from one end to the other. I remember self-seeding yellow verbascum in the gravel path fronting the border when we visited many years ago, but these tall plants are now confined to the rear, together with pink delphiniums.

The White Garden is now renamed the Well Garden, but still sports a preponderance of pale flowers. As well as white, there are now touches of cream from achillea and delphiniums the colour of custard, while *Eryngium* 'Miss Willmott's Ghost' interjects a steely, grey-blue note, and *Viola cornuta* in pure white is used as ground cover.

The Long Walk, which runs the whole length of the garden furthest away from the house, still has borders edged with box. Three iron arches give height and are covered in roses and clematis. The planting is of mixed shrubs and herbaceous perennials, mostly with a blue and yellow theme when we visited in July. In fact, every choice plant that one imagines can be found flowering at some time of the year at Wollerton. From the rare double delphinium in sky-blue, to *Eryngium alpinum* 'Amethyst' — a flower arranger's dream plant — to

globe artichokes and campanulas in every shade between dark blue and white.

Another favourite is the Font Garden. Very simple, with a centrepiece based on a sixteenth-century font surrounded by bulbs in rough grass, facing a loggia covered by a climbing rose. Further interest comes from clipped mounds of foliage, the whole providing a beautiful quiet space separate from the vibrant garden around.

Hot colours can be found in the area inspired by the Cornish garden of Lanhydrock. Here foliage is purple from *Cotinus coggygria*, copper beech, ligularia and a strongly growing vine decorating the walls. I noted red hot pokers, monarda and red salvias, a well as a stand of fabulous Turk's cap lilies in hot bronze. Later in the season dahlias come into their own, together with rudbeckias and heleniums.

One can only be awe-struck at the incredible attention to detail manifest throughout the entire garden at Wollerton. It is now a real show piece in every sense of the word, combining drama and design with a wonderful collection of plants.

The Wrekin Rose Garden · Eaton Constantine

A beautifully designed garden packed with plants and interesting features. Open for groups in season.

Please telephone: 01952 510714 for details

A visit to The Wrekin Rose Garden is an enlightening experience. As one walks around you begin to understand why it has won every competition that it has ever been entered for, from the local *Shropshire Star* Garden of the Year, to the nation-wide *Daily Mail* National Garden Competition. In fact, out of the twenty competitions entered, it has a clean sweep — and there were over two thousand entrants in the *Daily Mail* competition. The owners are romantics, indeed, with over three hundred roses in the garden, as well as many statues in marble and bronze, to say nothing of the glorious setting, it would be difficult to be anything else. One has no sensation of being high up on a hill, but the hedges have recently been lowered, and the views now stretch from the Stiperstones near Church Stretton to the Long Mynd.

The design of the main garden at the rear of the house appears simple, with undulating lawns falling away from the back of the house, wide borders around, and intricate paths covered in bark chips leading to shady areas hidden from view. The small front garden is mostly paved and boasts an original Abraham Darby kissing gate incorporated into the design, as well as a pond with a frog fountain full of Koi carp and goldfish.

The house and garden have been in the family for many years, but gardening proper only started about seventeen years ago. Nothing was drawn on paper as the owners have no truck with tape measures or worked out colour combinations, trusting to natural instincts and an eye for a good plant to see them through.

I was particularly impressed with the many original statues, all well placed at focal points — such as a bronze Perseus with Medusa's head on an ivy-covered plinth at the end of a pergola — or just peeping from among the foliage and flowers in the wide borders. A charming cockerel, his stone body a bird bath, marks the end of an island bed; while around a dark corner, down a narrow path, a bronze boy with a bucket

pours water into a barrel. The arrangement is very artless — a stone sink, a small trough with dianthus and erigeron, a variegated ivy and pretty, blue shaded grass — but perfectly placed to give interest in what could be a dull corner.

The soil in the garden is a free draining neutral loam, suitable for most herbaceous perennials. If acid lovers are planted, special planting material is used to bed them in, though the main mulch used is home made compost — the owners getting through three and a half tons per year. It seems to work, as I noted both *Rhododendron augustinii* and the difficult *R. amagianum*, both doing well.

The owners great love — apart from the roses — are day lilies or hemerocallis. These follow on well after the roses, filling the gaps with their exotic, trumpet-shaped blooms. Many new ones are added every year, including unusual varieties from America and Australia. These are often extremely expensive for just a tiny seedling and so are nursed in pots before being planted out into the main garden. Good advice for anyone who has doubts about the viability of a plant they have purchased.

As in all outstanding gardens, the owners have a policy of growing only the best. I was particularly drawn to a superior form of the old *Geranium wallichianum* 'Buxton's Blue', called 'Roseanne', with a much larger flower than the original plant. Maintenance of the plot is meticulous, as is the attention to detail throughout. For example, a weeping blue *Cedrus atlantica glauca* 'Pendula', is carefully pruned to fit its allotted position. Nearby, a

delightful 'brown' border, with roses, day lilies, *Berberis atropurpurea* 'Harlequin', and potentilla in subtle beige, or dark cream, all backed by *Sambucus nigra* 'Black Beauty', makes a unique colour combination.

Not that bright colour was wanting in the main borders when we visited in July, with blue spires of monkshood and delphiniums vying with the yellows and buffs of verbascums. Clematis are used to cover roses which have finished flowering, as well as decorating the house walls. Also close to the house are groups of self-sown *Papaver somniferum*, surely the biggest and most blousy of all the poppies, with show-stopping fully double blooms in wonderful shades of lavender and pink. One of the owners insists that she keeps pulling them up, but new ones appear every year, adding just the right note of informality.

I think that to create a successful garden, its gardener must have a dream, but few will fulfil it to quite the extent of the owners of The Wrekin Rose Garden.